CONTRARY TO CONCEPTION

STORIES AND LESSONS ABOUT SUCCESSFUL BIRTH CONTROL AND CONTRACEPTIVE METHODS

MADELINE V. PASIMIO, DDS

NEW DEGREE PRESS

COPYRIGHT © 2022 MADELINE V. PASIMIO, DDS

CONTRARY TO CONCEPTION

Stories and Lessons about Successful Birth Control and Contraceptive Methods

ISBN   979-8-88504-109-6   *Paperback*
         979-8-88504-750-0   *Kindle Ebook*
         979-8-88504-229-1   *Ebook*

CONTRARY TO CONCEPTION

Miriam, Edmund, Miko, Marcus, and Michael—kain na!

CONTENTS

INTRODUCTION

Sandy loved being a mother. Although motherhood came with taxing and worrisome hurdles over the years, she cherished pouring love into her two daughters, Jessie and Tahlia. Lately, Sandy enjoyed watching her daughters quickly sprout into young adults. Sandy adored this bond, selflessly sharing in their lives and gently planting seeds of wisdom when she could.

One evening, when her dad was not around, Jessie approached her mom, asking, "Will you take me to go see a doctor?"

Sandy's stomach lurched as she reflexively asked, "Is everything okay? What's wrong?"

Jessie hesitated, which was unusual for someone as confident as her.

"Please don't tell dad, but I want to go on birth control," she begged.

"Oh..."

Sandy felt a rush of shock yet a sense of comfort when she realized her daughter came to her with this request at all. Still, she was not prepared to have that conversation tonight. She was filled with endless questions but did not want her daughter to feel attacked.

Sandy replied, "Let's talk about it more this weekend."

Sandy stayed out in the living room with her laptop that night. She searched the internet for articles showing examples of birth control dialogues between a parent and child, and she checked her mom social media groups for threads on how these discussions went for others. She did not feel a strong connection to the tips listed online.

Sandy wondered if she should include her husband in this even though Jessie explicitly asked her not to. *How would I keep this a secret?* she thought. Her husband was in charge of their medical bills and was the type of person to really comb through mailed statements he did not recognize.

After all her searching, Sandy was at a loss for how to guide Jessie in this decision. Her own mother had not taught her about birth control, and she felt it would have been extremely awkward. Jessie was only fifteen years old, and that felt too young. *Would it be dangerous for Jessie's health if I started her on birth control already?* She had no idea how it really worked and hardly questioned the effects birth control had on herself, but now the stakes of not knowing felt drastically higher.

Her thoughts continued to spiral: *What am I supposed to do?*

***

Sandy and Jessie's story was inspired by a friend's true story. It highlights the confusing and daunting landscape of contraceptive knowledge. To Sandy's credit, when it comes to understanding birth control, many people admit they do not understand the intricacies of female anatomy and biological processes affected by these powerful drugs and devices.

According to survey data commissioned by The National Campaign to Prevent Teen Unplanned Pregnancy and conducted by the Guttmacher Institute, people interested in using birth control start their search with a few familiar methods, consulting media sources and possibly a few personal sources. Then they navigate the confusing healthcare system on their own, determining how to attain their method of choice (Kaye, Suellentrop, and Sloup, 2009). The problem compounds when another's life is involved as well, like a beloved daughter.

In my own culture (Filipino-American), talking about anything remotely sex-related is extremely uncomfortable and taboo. My parents still cover my eyes and lower the volume on the TV when a kissing scene comes up during a movie. I didn't even know what a period was until I got one! I can only imagine the fear in other people's experiences, in any culture, when they decide they want to start a contraceptive method for the first time.

With my conservative upbringing, sex education was not on my radar, and my school did not allow it. In eighth grade, I had a sexual purity course that ended with each of my classmates promising to abstain from sex until marriage, and it had a 0 percent success rate. My first exposure to sex education was at public high school, but it left me feeling ashamed of broaching these topics and fearful of consequences. In college, I learned the intricacies of female reproductive health as part of my biology major, yet the information presented left me wondering how to apply it.

I had no exposure to contraception resources until a college nurse expressed concern. I did not know enough about my options, and I had trouble separating science from hearsay. I felt ashamed and continued to put it off.

After I graduated from dental school, I started working with patients regularly, connecting with them on ways to take charge of their dental health through a preventive philosophy that works for their lifestyle rather than a reactive philosophy. One day, I realized it was time to apply my philosophy as a dental provider to the rest of my health.

Finally, I was ready to start my search for contraception.

When I started my journey, I felt lost as a woman. I am a dentist in the healthcare field who has been highly trained in health and science. Even with my background, choosing a method for myself was very difficult. A gaping disconnect felt oddly evident between my biological sciences education and my sexual education.

I researched the various contraceptive methods and realized I held on to many unfounded misconceptions. Initially, I felt overwhelmed and fearful of short and long-term effects, and I had let my conservative upbringing and shows like *The Handmaid's Tale* form my understanding of contraception. As I challenged these fallacies and shared my findings with others, I realized many of my friends (also with science backgrounds) held many of the same preconceived notions that I did.

My closest friends shared they would "just deal with" their side effects or give up on the process entirely without consulting anyone, not even their doctors. My own journey was filled with trials and side effects that negatively affected my health for years. We all felt we were abnormal and settled for the side effects that appeared. I found hardly any of us knew what was truly going on with our bodies, and hardly any of us were satisfied with our methods.

I noted the resounding themes of frustration, distrust, and inaction.

I set out on a personal journey to understand the options available, learn how people make these choices for themselves, and assess and communicate successful outcomes. Too often, we compromise our experience when it feels like we should be able to personalize our experience and find a solution that works well in our lifestyle.

Now, I am here to be a reliable friend who can share different outside experiences that showcase contraceptive methods in a familiar and approachable way. With a deeper connection to our bodies, we can better dictate the steps for our reproductive and overall health.

CONTRACEPTION TERMS

Contraception is used for various reasons, most often for **birth control**, intending to delay or prevent pregnancy. I most often refer to birth control as contraception, as the term **contraception** encompasses different motivations for using it.

I will discuss the contraceptive methods in this book in order of invasiveness, though the methods are often referred to in order of **effectiveness**. What makes a contraceptive method effective? In birth control terms, effectiveness is defined in the percentage of females who do not get pregnant within one year of starting a birth control method. If a method is 91 percent effective, this means about nine out of one hundred females using the method in a year may still get pregnant. Effectiveness is further broken down into perfect use and typical use.

- **Perfect use** is the level of effectiveness achieved when a method is used exactly as directed.
- **Typical use** accounts for human operator error, e.g., did not take the method on time or the method came out or fell off accidentally.

Success is another key term, the compatibility of a method for a person's lifestyle. For example, a person's birth control pill could be preventing pregnancy yet cause frequent migraines. While the pill effectively prevents pregnancy in this case, it unsuccessfully works into their life. Lack of success could eventually lead to decreased effectiveness as the user may feel less inclined to use their method.

Several contraceptive methods exist on the market today. The CDC lists them on their website:

- Birth control pills
    - Progestin-only pills ("mini-pills")
    - Combined oral contraceptives ("combo pills")
- Emergency contraception (EC)
- Barrier methods
    - Male condoms
    - Female condoms
    - The diaphragm
    - The sponge
    - The cap
    - Spermicides
- Withdrawal
- Fertility awareness-based methods
- The patch
- The ring
- Injectables (the shot)
- Long-acting reversible contraceptives (LARCs)
    - The implant
    - Hormonal intrauterine devices (IUDs)
    - The copper IUD

- Sterilization
  - Male vasectomy
  - Female tubal occlusion/ligation

Most people are not familiar with the various forms of contraception available, and most young people report awareness of only two to three methods (Kaye, Suellentrop, and Sloup, 2009).

THE CURRENT CONTRACEPTION LANDSCAPE

WHY IS CONTRACEPTION IMPORTANT?

Global development advocates champion family planning resources, notably providing contraception. Why?

<u>Health Benefits</u>
Contraception provides health benefits. It helps us prevent sexually transmitted infections. It provides safer pregnancy experiences. Contraception allows women to safely space out pregnancies, avoid pregnancy complications when they may be too young or too old, and reduce abortions from unintended pregnancies (WHO, 2019).

<u>Education and Economic Advantages</u>
Contraception allows people to make choices that may increase their status. Contraception can help women stay in school longer, increase earning potential, and plan resources adequately for their families. Investing in these spheres and using contraception as a tool can empower women to manage and advocate for their own

health. It allows them to plan their futures and direct their lives (Barot, 2017).

WHAT BARRIERS DO WE FACE?

<u>Personal Misconceptions and Fears</u>

Many females hold general health concerns about contraceptives that are important to investigate. They may worry about how contraceptives change their natural menstrual cycle and other biological rhythms, how contraceptives affect fertility, and how contraceptives impact their well-being. As a provider, it is important for me to identify when a patient's fears interfere with their desired outcomes.

Of the 6.1 million pregnancies in the US each year, 45 percent are unintended (Guttmacher, 2021). For some people, an unintended pregnancy can be the greatest joy of their life, giving them the precious child they did not anticipate. For some, an unintended pregnancy may be detrimentally inopportune, and they may prefer to delay—even terminate—pregnancy at all costs. In 2014, 51 percent of patients who had an abortion reported using contraception the month they became pregnant (Jones, 2018). Perhaps in these cases, contraception use may not have been adequately explained, understood, or used.

On an individual level, roughly 23 percent of women reported gaps in their contraceptive use when they preferred to delay pregnancy. Additionally, 24 percent report switching their contraceptive within a year. Switching contraceptives over the course of a year can result in inconsistent contraceptive use (Frost, Singh, and Finer, 2007). This may signal some potential issues. Perhaps these people were not satisfied with their chosen method and used contraceptives inconsistently.

Furthermore, 19 percent of sexually active women seeking to avoid pregnancy are not using contraception (Kaye, Suellentrop, and Sloup, 2009). These women share various reasons for the lack of consistent contraceptive use. Some report infrequent sexual activity and were not prepared when the time came. Some blame prior negative contraception experiences (Frost, Singh, and Finer, 2007). They may not be aware of how to use contraception to their advantage, they may be "just dealing with" side effects until it becomes unacceptable, or they may not realize they have options.

Many people fear the repercussions a contraceptive may have on their health. The conversation of contraception involves confusingly integrated topics of biology, lifestyle considerations, healthy relationships, mental and emotional experiences, and finances. These decisions can feel impossibly difficult and isolating at times.

Rather than continue this journey alone, I believe we can help contraception users improve their experience. To reduce these gaps and increase satisfaction with contraception, we need to identify the problems they face. With a comprehensive understanding, we can build realistic expectations and collaborate on a plan that meets their needs.

As we explore examples and stories, it can bring comfort and familiarity to understand how contraception works and what successful methods can look like.

Education Disparities

When a person starts to consider a contraceptive method, how do they build their foundational knowledge? Can they (and should they) rely on their friends for information? How about internet media? Like Jessie, unmarried young adults report getting their primary contraception information from the media (35 percent) or a personal source (34 percent) rather than a doctor or professional source. Furthermore, when learning about a new contraceptive method, 52 percent of them report they would consult the media first (Kaye, Suellentrop, and Sloup, 2009).

I feel it is fortunate Jessie had a trusting relationship with her mom to ask her when she could have gone to an unreliable source.

So what role does sex education in schools play in this conversation?

Reproductive health is a subject not comfortably talked about, educated on, or practically addressed since society still perpetuates negative stigmas on promiscuity. Furthermore, a patchwork of educational resources in schools exist where only thirty states and the District of Columbia mandate sex education, and only twenty states and DC are currently required to include contraception information in those courses (Guttmacher, 2022). If we look at that sample of unmarried young adults, they report not having recent, quality sexual education. If 71 percent of young adults report receiving sex education when they were sixteen or younger (27 percent say they were fourteen or younger), how can we counter the spread and belief of misinformation (Kaye, Suellentrop, and Sloup, 2009)?

Negative social pressures in today's culture seep discomfort into mere conversations of periods, PAP smears, and uteruses. Our current climate keeps some people ashamed of having these conversations and fearful of associating themselves with sexual promiscuity (Sully et al., 2020). As a result, they may choose not to use a contraceptive method altogether when they would prefer to (Dreweke, 2019). The problem with shame is it creates a culture of secrecy. Some women wonder how to choose contraceptives but feel ashamed to voice their questions, and some question their experience, unsure if a solution exists. On top of the complex emotional strife that accompanies this shame, these women may be left figuring out their health concerns for themselves, or even ignoring it completely (Dreweke, 2019).

I believe education is a key part of addressing negative stigma. Not until we have medically accurate and comprehensive information available to all young people will we see a true change in ownership over sexual health (Schroeder et al., 2022).

<u>Opposition to Access</u>

The reproductive age of women is roughly between fifteen and forty-four years old, and over 99 percent of women have reported using contraception at some point during these years. The average American woman claims to want only two children of relatively close age to one another (Guttmacher, 2021). That leaves roughly twenty-five years' worth of pregnancies to prevent.

While the demand for contraception is high, counterintuitively, some people have difficulty attaining it. This signals possible system-wide problems. Across the US, varying degrees of contraceptive access are available. Federal mandates require contraceptive coverage; however, recent political loopholes have been enacted to allow organizations to refuse coverage on moral or religious grounds. Although contraception is central to health and economic success, funding to contraceptive service clinics has been reduced nationally.

To complicate the mix, states have various exemptions further limiting which methods are covered, minors' access to contraception, and minors' ability to consent for health services. Frustratingly, there is no way to clearly and concisely answer questions of access and coverage; it depends on individual company policies and state laws. (For more information on state-specific coverage and regulations, see the Resource section.)

My heart goes out to those young people, like Jessie, trying to grasp their biology, relationships (family, friend, and romantic), and safety while navigating the healthcare system. Policies limit their autonomy (ability to make decisions over their health concerns) and deny their anonymity (desire to keep their medical decisions only between them and the people they choose). Society pushes for advancements in all sectors yet leaves many young people disjointed in their sexual identities. While many young persons do come out of their situations empowered through self-directed research and guidance from their communities, many do not.

Lack of contraceptive knowledge creates fatigue and dissatisfaction, and people give up exploring more options. After several negative experiences compound, a sense of hopelessness remains, and a fear no contraceptive method could possibly satisfy their lifestyle lingers. While all these above factors play a role in the storm of confusion surrounding contraception, to me, the heart of it stems from the broken message and distorted purpose of sexuality.

Sexuality is an inherent and beautiful part of being human. Sex can be skewed to gain power, create stigma, and divide. Instead, maybe if sex was seen as part of a fulfilling and responsible life, we could abandon fears of it corrupting our society. Perhaps we could then fully equip women with control over their bodies.

PUTTING IT ALL TOGETHER

I want others to feel like they have the resources they need to make this decision openly. I believe an accurate and comprehensive understanding is essential to making the best decisions for health. My hope is this book can help those of reproductive age consider their contraceptive options from a reliable perspective. This could also be a helpful resource for aiding others in making this decision, perhaps a child, a patient, or a friend.

The content in this book is for informational and educational purposes only. It is not intended as medical advice. Instead, I am sharing what I have learned throughout my journey and providing examples of what others have gone through. However, everyone is different. It is important to work with a partnering doctor, and we will go into examples of how to do that. Medical advice from a qualified healthcare professional, I hope, will be a central part in choosing a method.

Contraception can provide reliable birth control, especially for those who do not desire to grow their family (for a period of time or forever). It can also alleviate various female reproductive system health concerns. Knowing how to best stay safe, healthy, and in control are important reasons to enter this dialogue as soon as reasonably possible.

Understanding all our options is the first step. Most people are not familiar with most options or their unknown effects on the body. Throughout this book, we will explore how they work, associated side effects, and ways to evaluate success. We will also encounter true events experienced by real people (all names have been changed to protect their privacy) who have had their own set of unique yet relatable experiences. They are a culmination of various stories I received through personal interviews and public videos.

We will hear from women like PhD student Gina, who learned to control her severe cramps; college student Vera, who navigated contraceptive resources in a brand-new city; and Terri, who, with her partner David, collaborated on a contraceptive choice. With these stories and more, shared personal experiences, and supporting research, maybe we can take our health into our own hands, living free of pain and fear stemming from these ovarian and uterine mysteries.

Once on our journey, perhaps we can all join in on sharing stories and lessons to expose reproductive health stigmas and embrace an enriching path forward.

SETTING THE STAGE

KEY TERMS AND DEFINITIONS

In this section, we will briefly go over terms that frequently appear in this book.

First, an important acknowledgment in the topic of contraception revolves around terms like *woman* and *female*. A person's sex tends to denote anatomical or physical traits at birth, e.g., *male* and *female*. A person's gender differs and includes their identity—how they express themselves in terms of societal roles, e.g., *woman* and *girl* (Michael S. Kimmel, *The Gendered Society*, 2000). I acknowledge these terms have limitations while our world consists of diverse sex and gender identities. For this book, when we evaluate how contraception affects the human body, I will use the terms **male** and **female** to represent a person's assigned sex at birth. I refer to **men** and **women** when a particular study asks how subjects identify or if a social sense is assumed, but I attempt to refer to **people** as much as possible when applicable as all individuals may be included in contraception decisions.

When talking about contraception, another distinction between methods is their ability to protect against **sexually transmitted infections (STIs)**. According to the Office on Women's Health website article "Sexually transmitted infections," STIs can spread between partners when having vaginal, oral, or anal sex. The only way to prevent all types of STIs is to not have sex (abstinence). When having sex, several steps can help lower the risk, but they are not 100 percent effective: vaccination, condoms, frequent testing, and limiting sex partners. Most contraceptive options do not protect against STIs.

ANATOMICAL TERMS

To build knowledge about contraception, we can start by laying a foundation of the biological processes occurring in the internal female reproductive system. Hormonal contraception acts on this system to activate natural biological defenses to prevent pregnancy or to create desired physical outcomes. Non-hormonal methods typically rely on physical barriers to physically block the start of pregnancy. Some also help prevent STIs. Defining physical anatomy is important to understand how these methods work.

Think back to (or look up) an image of the iconic ram-shaped female reproductive organs. It is made up of a central tube (the ram's head) and two diverting tubes (the ram's horns), with oval pouches on the ends.

The oval pouches are the **ovaries**, containing individual **eggs**, female genetic code. The diverting tubes leading toward the central tube are the **fallopian tubes,** where one egg travels down each month (**ovulation**) and where it can meet a **sperm**, male genetic code.

The central tube has a constriction in the middle, separating it into a lower tube and an upper tube. The lower tube is the **vagina** (the vaginal canal), where tampons, fingers, and penises can be housed. The upper tube is the **uterus**, the place where (1) the **embryo** (the united sperm and egg) can embed (or implant) in the walls to form a baby or (2) the uterus walls can shed and start the menstrual cycle (a person's period). The constriction between is the **cervix,** which can be blocked (by a contraceptive) to prevent sperm from reaching deeper into the system.

The sperm and egg have a finite lifespan. While the egg lives for only twelve to twenty-four hours, sperm can actually survive three to five days within a female's reproductive system (Office on Women's Health, 2018). In other words, even if sex occurs before egg release, sperm can wait around to meet the egg. This is important to remember, as the timing of the contraceptive method used plays a crucial role in its effectiveness.

MENSTRUAL CYCLE TERMS

Approximately every month, if a female is not pregnant, they have a **period** or they **menstruate.** The start of the menstrual cycle is when the uterus sheds its lining. The lining makes it way down from the uterus, past the cervix and vagina, and expels itself as period bleeding. Typical periods last for about four to eight days (Office on Women's Health, 2018).

During a person's period, the uterus releases signals to induce strong muscle contractions (or **"cramps"**) to shed the lining (Ray, DNP, 2021). Some people suffer from severely painful cramps and/or period bleeding problems due to underlying female reproductive system issues such as **endometriosis**, uterine fibroids, adenomyosis, and polycystic ovarian syndrome (**PCOS**). In women of reproductive age, endometriosis is prevalent in about 10 to 15 percent (Giudice and Kao, 2004), while PCOS is prevalent in 5 to 20 percent (Azziz et al., 2016). This is important to consider, as these symptoms could be motivations people identify for using contraception other than birth control.

Contraception often affects a person's period, sometimes lessening bleeding or creating the absence of bleeding (Rodriguez, 2015). Some hormonal contraceptives have a higher association with light **breakthrough bleeding** (bleeding between periods). Obstetrician and Gynecologist (OBGYN) experts, like Dr. Valerie French, assure contraceptive-related breakthrough bleeding "rarely signals a health problem" (French, MD, 2021).

Some people feel the body needs to have a period every month as a "cleanse." However, the body does not menstruate when it is "dirty." It menstruates to prepare for pregnancy. Only ten primate species—elephant shrews, bats, and spiny mice—outwardly menstruate. Instead, other animals reabsorb these tissues inconspicuously (Blackman, 2017).

Since humans experience periods so vividly, we may rely on them to provide the security we are not pregnant.

According to the American Pregnancy Association, some pregnant people experience **amenorrhea** (no period bleeding). However, some may still have **spotting** (light period bleeding), which may appear like a fairly normal period. Therefore, periods may not necessarily be the most reliable way to confirm pregnancy status. Instead, a pregnancy test can be used or a doctor can be consulted.

HORMONE TERMS

Hormones are important to understanding contraception, as many contraceptive methods work using a hormonal pathway. Side effects that appear are related to these pathways.

Hormones are a specific type of molecule secreted in one part of the body that signals another body part to act (even itself). All hormones have a similar base structure, which is why they are in the same category. Furthermore, low doses of hormones can create one outcome, and high doses of the same hormone can create a completely opposite outcome. Isn't the human body amazing?

Different ways to categorize hormones exist. **Testosterone** is the major **androgen** (male sex hormone) that promotes and maintains male sex characteristics. Testosterone in higher doses can cause hair growth, acne, weight gain, and increased sex drive (SEER, 2022).

Estrogen and **progesterone** are the major female sex hormones. Estrogen in higher doses can cause breast development and fat production (SEER, 2022). Progesterone in higher levels can increase appetite and sleepiness, which females tend to experience in the latter half of their menstrual cycle (Lopez et al., 2016). Both these hormones signal many other effects too.

Most hormonal contraceptive methods use **progestin**, synthetic progesterone. Progestin is the central ingredient that gives us four major effects of birth control and contraception:

1. In the menstrual cycle, high levels of progesterone tell the body it has already ovulated. Consistently high levels of progestin signal to the brain it is *not* time to release an egg (ovulation is prevented). No egg, no pregnancy.
2. Another bonus of progestin is the thickening of the cervical mucus within the cervix (constricted canal between the vagina and the uterus). This "mucus plug" blocks sperm from getting into or past the uterus. No sperm and egg union, no pregnancy.
3. Even in the unlikely event a sperm made it through this mucus plug, its motility would be completely ruined and unable to reach the egg. No sperm motility, no pregnancy.
4. Lastly, progestin thins the uterus' lining. In the unlikelier event a sperm and egg met, they would have a difficult time embedding into the lining (implanting) to even start the pregnancy process. No implantation, no pregnancy.

An important note for this definition choice is that although these are considered male or female hormones,

these hormones are typically found in all people at dif-
fering levels (Edwards and Can, 2021).

***

As we explore topics that build on these ideas, it could be helpful to refer to this section in case terms need clarification.

HISTORY

As we often question throughout formal education, what is the importance of history? Historical events and movements shape our systems and influence our conceptions. Stepping back and contemplating our (possibly outdated) assumptions is important when making choices in the present, especially when it comes to our health.

This book is not meant to be an in-depth analysis of birth control history nor its impacts on society. Instead, the focus is to explore the pertinent historical events that influence the misconceptions that may be hindering us from selecting or using contraception.

EARLY BIRTH CONTROL METHODS

We typically think of the popular birth control pill as one of the first contraceptive methods available. However, contraceptive methods have been around since the ancient world.

Early contraceptive methods share striking resemblances with some of our current ones. We find recipes of natural concoctions that decreased male and female fertility, chemical solutions (like fruit juice, vinegar, oil) that killed sperm, and recorded items (like rocks and sponges) inserted into the vagina to block the uterus. Attempts to track female fertility rhythms have been documented (although inaccurately until the 1920s), and perhaps some of the oldest methods still used today were abstinence and withdrawal methods (Engelman, 2011).

These discoveries hint at a pattern of humans seeking to control reproduction.

In early nomadic civilizations, birth control methods were used often, as it was easier to care for smaller family sizes. During agricultural revolutions, families could stay rooted in the land they cultivated. In these contexts, it was advantageous to have larger families collectively work farmlands together, making birth control practices less popular. This latter phenomenon was illustrated in the 1700s, when the average woman had about eight live births. During industrialization in the 1800s, we see this average drop to three live births when large families were more difficult to support economically. Although not openly advertised, the rapid change in family size was due to birth control (Gordon, 2002).

INFLUENCES ON THE BIRTH CONTROL MOVEMENT

VICTORIAN IDEOLOGIES (EARLY 1800S TO LATE 1800S)

The birth control movement was shaped in response to the Victorian Era's religious and moral standards of regality and sexual purity (Independence Hall Association, 2022). These ideologies unfairly subjected women to a "dainty" and "fair" culture of femininity in order to define and divide gender roles.

Sexual pleasure was unwomanly and sinful, sex was only allowed in marriage, and abstinence was the only acceptable contraceptive. Women during this time had unease and unfamiliarity with their own bodies, staying clothed during sexual intercourse and even washing themselves with their garments still worn (Gordon, 2002).

Although women were a major aspect of the workforce before marriage, their ultimate destiny was motherhood. Women were conditioned to be physically weaker, confined indoors and subjected to poor working and living conditions. Women were expected to care for their household; men were expected to work long hours outside the home. These gender roles kept women economically dependent on their husbands during this time. This limited women's status and often kept them subordinate to men (Price et al., 2014).

The Comstock laws of 1873 highlight these ideologies. They prevented the mailed distribution of "obscene or immoral" materials, and they prohibited abortion and contraceptives, even for married couples. Defying these laws resulted in fines, jail time, and often public defamation (Tone, 2001).

While these regulations were imposed to enforce sexual morality, we find accounts of women acting out of desperation to control their bodies; contraceptive use continued in an underground fashion. Creative code words had to be used to inform women where abortions could take place and contraceptives could be acquired. Often these unofficial abortions were dangerous and unsterile, resulting in serious infection. Although the consequences of acting out these illegal activities could result in incarceration, social ruin, and even death, women still sought out contraception and abortions. Attempts to stamp out sexual knowledge and resources instead created unsafe health conditions, especially in the poorest groups that could not obtain contraception (Gordon, 2002).

The birth control movement ultimately saved women's lives. It directed society toward destigmatizing these preconceived sexual values and toward gender equality.

NATURAL SELECTION AND EUGENICS

During the mid-19th century, Charles Darwin published his work on the natural selection of populations, and Gregor Mendel published his work on principles of inherited traits. These discoveries were at the forefront scientifically, where, in nature, inferior populations die out as more fit and superior populations reproduce, passing down their genes to future generations (Gordon, 2002). These ideas were manipulated to justify various oppressions.

The largely undiscussed history of birth control took a grim turn during the late nineteenth century as the eugenics movement gained traction. The eugenics movement was the suppression of "undesirable gene traits" (e.g., dark skin, disabilities, mental disorders). As minority populations grew in numbers, the eugenics movements sought to limit non-white races (Gordon, 2002). Even famed president Theodore Roosevelt was an outspoken eugenicist, vindicating, "[S]ociety has no business to permit degenerates to reproduce their kind" (Roosevelt, 1913). Forced sterilizations and non-consensual contraceptive treatments ultimately resulted in further oppression of groups like the Black community, Native Americans, and Puerto Ricans.

During the Progressive Era (1890s to 1920s), the women's rights movement spurred the popular idea of "voluntary motherhood" as a retaliation against Victorian values. For the birth control movement to gain traction in this sex-negative culture, its pioneers partnered with the eugenics movement (Gordon, 2002).

DRUG SAFETY IN THE PROGRESSIVE ERA

In the early twentieth century, medical drugs could be released for widespread use in the US without regulations requiring standardized clinical testing or trials (US FDA, 2019). In 1937, a deadly antibiotic (containing a toxic component of antifreeze) was released on the market, killing over a hundred people, including children, as soon as it was released. This was the ultimate tipping point leading to the passing of the Food, Drug, and Cosmetic Act of 1938, creating foundational drug safety checks (US FDA, Nov 2018).

Scientific standards followed years later with the passing of the Drug Amendments of 1962 when thalidomide (a treatment for morning sickness that ended up causing birth defects) started becoming popular in the US (Ballentine, 1981). These standards ensured drug benefits outweighed risks, clinical trials required informed consent, and accurate drug advertising included side effects (US FDA, Feb 2018). Through tragedy, FDA approval was born.

To bring the first contraceptive method, the pill, to market, researchers had to prove the efficacy and safety of the pill to the FDA. However, it took years to refine these laws into the standards we have today. Now, various safeguards exist to keep citizens safe from drugs on the market. Contraceptive methods on the market today are subjected to much more rigorous standards.

THE BIRTH CONTROL MOVEMENT

"Enforced motherhood is the most complete denial of a woman's right to life and liberty."

—MARGARET SANGER

Birth control advocate and eugenicist Margaret Sanger is credited with the legalization of the pill and the founding of Planned Parenthood. Ultimately, she believed that if women could control their reproduction, then it would lead to their social and economic equality (Michals, 2017).

As FDA safety regulations were now in place, clinical trials were needed to prove this first form of the pill was effective. Sanger worked with a team consisting of reproductive studies biologists Gregory Pincus, John Rock, and M.C. Chang, as well as investor/philanthropist Katharine McCormick, to launch human clinical trials on women in Puerto Rico. Although the women taking part in this study were informed they were taking a contraceptive, they were not told the drug was experimental. Side effects of dizziness and nausea ran rampant during these trials, and, in some cases, women were involuntary sterilized. Furthermore, three women in the trials died due to the extremely high doses of the hormones given in these trials (twenty times the hormone dose used in pills today) (PPFA, 2022).

These trials did lead to the FDA approval of the first birth control pill available on the US market in 1960. Sadly, complications of blood clots were numerous. Still, the product was highly desired, especially during the Great Depression, when families could not afford to get too large due to financial constraints (PPFA, 2015).

Although it has atrocious ties to eugenics, the birth control pill in recent times is more positively associated with a breadth of female empowerment. Now, the pill is the most common reversible form of birth control in the US. About one in four contraceptive users (over 9.5 million women) choose the pill as their method (Guttmacher, 2021).

Birth control and contraception became widely sought-after products that continued to develop into the more sophisticated and effective forms we have today.

PUTTING IT ALL TOGETHER

Throughout history, the media negatively portrayed contraceptive methods as defective and loosely regulated medical devices that caused harm. However, those products are no longer found on the market. For example, a poorly designed IUD called the Dalkon Shield was prevalent and harmfully affected many females in the 1970s to 1980s (Hubacher, 2002). We will go into more detail on this event in future chapters. Current rigorous standards of FDA approval can help us restore some faith in medical drugs and devices available in the US.

Again, integrated and complex historical events are crucial to a complete understanding of our current contraceptive climate, and the information presented here provides a stepping stone. We will investigate some of these important events and movements further. But, for those interested, I have included a list of reading materials in the Resource section that can help provide a more profound understanding.

In making contraception decisions, we must learn from its harmful, divisive history and instead make positive, inclusive choices. As a silver lining, hormonal contraception came to light as we know it today after this radical time in history.

Since targeted communities were subjected to contraception unknowingly, certain populations may still reject the idea of particular contraceptive methods, harboring negative and appalling associations. This is important to know in helping others make a decision about contraception. Although people should be informed of all their options, providers or others sharing information on these methods need to be aware of possible reasons for pushback.

No contraception method is without side effects, and side effects can be serious. However, the general concern of side effects tends to be overestimated. The safety of available contraceptive methods has been tested and approved for most people. In subsequent chapters, we will dive into the research and data detailing the safety of each method.

Now, many famed global development philanthropists, like the Bill and Melinda Gates Foundation, highlight how the empowering of women through contraception promotes equality and subsequently brings about wealth and success to those countries. Reproductive control is fundamentally desired; it can help us shape more successful futures.

PART 2

THE MAIN EVENT (THE METHODS)

THE PILL

Gina grew up as a responsible, bright, and secure child. She was self-motivated and confident, yet nurturing and humble. She felt accepted by her witty older brothers and loving parents. Her family relied on her to spearhead gatherings, where she would happily volunteer to plan meals and activities, and she joyfully helped tutor classmates if they asked for additional help or notes. True to her nature, she continually proved to be unconditionally sweet and pleasant.

As tempting as it might be to assume she was perfect, Gina was still human, and she struggled with aggravating period cramps. They were so debilitating that she had to stay in bed every month for one to two days in order to cope. When these days fell on school days, she would feel discouraged and behind since she loved learning. Finally, at the age of twenty-five, during the start of her PhD program, she felt she could no longer afford to take precious time off and wanted to take ownership of her health and body.

She had just moved to a new city and did not have anyone to ask for a doctor's recommendation. She decided to find a medical doctor covered by her parent's insurance. On the insurance website, Dr. Nguyen seemed knowledgeable, hardworking, and compassionate.

When Gina found herself in Dr. Nguyen's consultation room, he welcomed her, saying, "Hi, Gina, I'm Dr. Nguyen. How are you?"

She said, "Hi, Dr. Nguyen. Nice to meet you. Honestly, I feel a bit awkward, I guess?"

"This is a vulnerable space. I decided to go into medicine twenty years ago because I felt the desire to live a long healthy life connects us together. I'm here to help people achieve that in any way I can," Dr. Nguyen said.

Gina felt more at ease. "Well, I'm currently in school, and it's one of the most stressful times of my life. I've been dealing with very painful cramps for over ten years, and it's gotten to the point where I'm tired of missing school or interrupting my research to sleep off my pain. I'm interested in using contraception to help. What do you think?"

As she spoke, Dr. Nguyen was already considering this as an option but first asked, "Have you tried other pain management methods? Like heating pads, changing your diet, or exercise?"

"I've tried all those in the past. They would help reduce the pain sometimes but not enough to get me to function normally on extremely painful days, even in combination," she explained.

He agreed she could try going on *the pill* to help.

Dr. Nguyen started Gina on a "mini-pill" and informed her this was a low-risk way to start since it did not contain estrogen. Estrogen would put her at a higher risk of blood clots and other health issues. He also informed her that although it worked well to prevent pregnancy, it had a narrow window of effectiveness, meaning they needed to be taken at the same time every day. Since Gina was not using the pill specifically to prevent pregnancy during this time, she accepted this recommendation.

On the same day, Gina conveniently picked up her medication from the medical center's in-house pharmacy and did not have to pay any out-of-pocket costs. She eagerly opened the packet and examined its contents. The pack of medication contained four rows of pink pills, twenty-eight pills total. The pharmacist who dispensed the medication instructed her to consume one pill every day at the same time. He warned her, "These pills do not protect against sexually transmitted infections or diseases."

After a few months on this drug, Gina's world changed. Her cramps were more manageable, and she could function in the same way she felt other women did while on their periods. However, her period was happening all the time, inconveniencing her when she took trips, and giving her acne when she thought these pills worked to get rid of acne. This negatively affected her self-confidence.

She consulted her doctor to see if he could change her regimen. He suggested a low-dose estrogen pill.

Gina waited three more months for the side effects to change, and, well, they changed alright. As expected, her period was more regulated, but she noticed a less desirable change, too. Gina had always had more peach fuzz on her body than most of her other girlfriends, but she realized her peach fuzz was getting darker—even on her face! Although most people could not tell, this experience horrified her, and she attributed it to the contraceptive pill.

Consulting with her doctor once more, she asked if anything more could be done. Was she just imagining symptoms, or was the issue caused by her schoolwork on top of all the stress she was dealing with? Dr. Nguyen informed her it could take several iterations of trial and error to get to the right form of pill that worked for her body. If she was willing to try out another, he could not guarantee what side effects she might experience, but with patience, she might find a solution that worked for her. She agreed, and he prescribed her a high-dose estrogen pill.

After a few more months on this new method, her period was more regulated and her cramps subsided. However, her mood felt off and her friends noticed she was not as cheerful as she normally was. School was taking more of a toll on her, and she suffered from intense migraines. Her vision blurred, and she would see flashes of light clouding her vision.

Her colleague took considerable notice during those months and asked, "Hey Gina, you seem really down these days. Is everything okay?"

She shyly responded, "Oh, I think I've just been exhausted from my research expectations. I'll feel a lot better after I get more conclusive data, but thanks for asking." She hastily turned and walked away. Unsure what to do next, she discontinued contraception altogether and hoped her severe period cramps would not return.

***

Although this story is a fictionalized accumulation of real friends' experiences, Gina's journey showcases several recurring themes. Many women strive to achieve balanced overall health yet are limited by their contraception side effects. This compounds when their reproductive system reacts in complicated ways. It can be difficult to grapple with the emotional toll of unfamiliarity with these medications and bodily changes.

To understand what happened to Gina, let's dive into the mechanisms of *the pill*.

HOW IT WORKS

Gina was aware she had to get a prescription in order to get access to the pill, and she was covered by her parent's medical insurance, so cost was not a deterrent. After her doctor's appointment, she simply went to her local pharmacy to pick it up. Without insurance, individuals may have partial or full coverage through certain state government plans (more information on this can be found in the Resource section). Contraceptive health service clinics (like Planned Parenthood and certain pharmacies) typically have these in stock, but the exact type of pill they may have available on a given day can vary (Bedsider, 2019). The types of pills stocked are an important consideration, as each pill can have different effects on different individuals.

Progestin-Only Pills (Mini-Pills)

Although we refer to birth control pills as "the pill," hundreds of birth control pills are on the market. But what is in these pills? Some pills contain progestin only, aka mini-pills. These pills typically come in twenty-eight-day packs of pills all the same color, meaning each pill contains the active progestin hormone (Roland and Carter, 2019).

A person taking these pills daily would create a constantly high level of progestin in their body. This would prevent egg release and create a mucus plug in the female reproductive system (Cooper and Mahdy, 2021).

Combined Oral Contraceptives (Combo Pills)

The more popular pills on the market contain a progestin combined with synthetic estrogen, or combination oral contraceptives, aka combo pills. A common layout for these pills would contain three weeks of the active hormone-containing pills, and the final week of the month would either contain one week of sugar pills (twenty-eight-day packs) or no pills for seven days (twenty-one-day packs). During the sugar pill or no pill phase, period bleeding typically occurs (PPFA, 2005).

Combo pills can also come in packs with a several-month supply. Extended-cycle birth control pill forms allow women to have four periods a year safely. These packs can be given all at once, providing users with eighty-four pills plus seven sugar pills (ninety-one-day packs). Again, the exact number of active (hormone-containing) pills and inactive (no hormone) pills varies between different brands (PPFA, 2005).

The main purpose of estrogen is to reduce unwanted side effects of pure progestin. Estrogen stabilizes the uterus lining and maintains regular menstrual cycle rhythms. In other words, women tend to experience more predictable periods (PPFA, 2005).

Combo pills can have varying amounts of progestin and estrogen in each pill—multiphasic. Natural cycles have a gradual rise and fall of hormone levels, and multiphasic combo pills attempt to mimic those levels. Other types of combo pills contain the same amount of hormones in each pill, monophasic (Mona et al., 2021).

Multiphasic pills give more control over period timing and can help users safely delay their period if they like.

Some people report an increase in breakthrough bleeding (bleeding between periods) when a period is delayed too long. A good rule of thumb is to allow at least four periods a year to help prevent uncontrolled spotting. Generally, the lower the amount of estrogen in the pill, the more likely breakthrough bleeding occurs (French, MD, 2013).

Although the pill can provide many benefits, it does not provide any protection against STIs (sexually transmitted diseases).

With all these different types, forms, and concoctions of birth control pills, people can set goals to achieve their desired reproductive outcomes. Some people like predictably knowing when their period will start and end; certain forms of the pill can give them this control. Sharing goals with a doctor can help the doctor select a pill that best addresses concerns.

EFFECTIVENESS

If this method is used timely and regularly, overall effectiveness is quite high, at 99.7 percent, and taking a pill each day feels more approachable and less invasive for people on this method. However, we see effectiveness drop to 93 percent with typical use (Bedsider, 2019).

When the pill regimen is first started, a female's reproductive system needs time to acclimate to the new hormone levels and begin signaling a change in the body. The effectiveness of the birth control pill is not immediately achieved for a few days (up to a week). A doctor can help determine the exact window depending on the pill selected. During the time it takes the pill to ramp up its effectiveness, either vaginal sex should be avoided or an additional method should be used to effectively prevent pregnancy (Taylor, 2020).

The main drawback is the pill *must* be taken daily at the same time every day or the possibility of unintended pregnancy increases. Life happens. Is it the end of the world if one little pill is forgotten? It may be cliché, but it depends. First and foremost, consult with a doctor based on the specific type of pill prescribed to be sure of what to do next.

The mini-pill (progestin-only) has an especially narrow window of effectiveness (twenty-three hours) and *must* be taken every day at the same time. If not, the effectiveness drops drastically and another form of contraception (emergency contraception and/or barrier method) should be implemented as a backup if sex occurs during this time (Jackson, MD, Andrea, 2011).

Again, keep in mind the fact that sperm can live within the female reproductive system for up to five days, so if a pill is also forgotten within five days of vaginal sex, emergency contraception would be the only backup method available (further information on emergency contraception will be provided later).

In practice, life can get in the way at the exact time the user may need to take their pill. For those who feel this pill routine would not be a good fit for their lifestyle, contraceptives that do not rely as much on the user should be considered.

SIDE EFFECTS

While not consistent among all birth control pill users, side effects are commonly reported. To understand where side effects stem from, we must further deepen our understanding of progestin. As a review, progestin is a synthetic form of the normally occurring hormone progesterone.

Although birth control pills are described to have progestin, the actual molecular structure between progestins among different brands varies. Not only do these individual molecules differ from one another, but also, they can resemble other molecules. Importantly, some progestins can more closely resemble other androgens like testosterone. This is where the difference in side effects experienced by users comes from (Darney, 1995).

To reduce unwanted side effects, drug developments comprise different strategies. Newer forms of progestins have been developed to reduce their similarity to androgens in order to avoid associated undesirable side effects. Additionally, hormone doses and ratios within different pills are balanced to counteract side effects. Research has shown these new formulations help people stick to their birth control regimen and experience birth control more positively (Jones, 1995). A medical provider can help determine which pills are associated with which types and generations of progestins.

Next, we can go into more specific examples of the pill's various side effects:

- Weight gain
- Migraines (with aura)
- Libido changes
- Acne
- Mood changes
- Rare cardiovascular problems

<u>Weight Gain</u>

Weight gain is a commonly associated side effect, as high levels of progestin increase appetite and sleepiness. On average, about four pounds (two kilograms) of weight gain has been reported in studies, but the research is limited. People using progestin-only pills document increased body fat composition and decreased lean body mass compared to people using non-hormonal contraceptives. Typically, most pill users can adjust to appetite changes associated with the pill over the course of a year (Lopez et al., 2016).

<u>Migraines (with Aura)</u>

As Gina experienced, a prevalent and noteworthy side effect of combination pills is migraines with aura. Migraines are painfully intense headaches that may blur vision, heighten sensitivity to light and sound, and induce nausea. Aura intensifies these symptoms up to an hour before migraine onset, such as visual zigzags or flashing spots, auditory or speech problems, and muscle weakness (American Migraine, 2017).

If already suffering from migraines, estrogen from combo pills can exacerbate them. The incidence of migraines with aura increases as a person using birth control ages, especially when they are over thirty-five years old. Additionally, headaches, upset stomachs, and nausea have been reported when using the pill. A tip to try to help avoid these symptoms is to take the pill right before bed, so the worst of these side effects passes while asleep (Edlow, MD, MSc and Bartz, MD, MPH, 2010).

Libido Changes

People using the pill often report a change in libido (sex drive) after starting the pill and when coming off the pill. High libido is associated with higher estrogen levels. When progesterone is more dominant, libido tends to be lower. Decreased libido is reported more with the progestin-only pills since natural estrogen levels are minimized (Bedsider, 2019).

Acne

Estrogen affects acne. High estrogen is associated with less acne, high progesterone is associated with more acne. Progestin-only pills may increase acne, while high estrogen combo pills may decrease acne. The FDA has approved certain brands of the pill to also treat acne, and if aware of their patient's acne concerns, doctors can provide additional information on these particular pills (Silver, 2022).

Mood Changes

Mood changes are a reported symptom that can be tough to measure. For some people, mood disorders may have an underlying reproductive system issue like premenstrual dysphoric disorder (PMDD), and the pill can be used to help treat it. In others, the effects on mood are not as well understood (Robakis et al., 2019). With heightened levels of progestin, mood tends to be similar to moods before a period but possibly tempered positively with estrogen. Again, this is a difficult symptom to predict or measure, and more specific research studies should be conducted to assess this (Lewis et al., 2019).

Rare Side Effects

Considering the importance of overall health, we cannot ignore the fine print. Combo pills containing estrogen include a very, very small risk of cardiovascular problems, like high blood pressure and blood clots, which can increase stroke risk (Office on Women's Health, 2019). However, pregnancy comes with a high risk of these complications as well. In comparison, the risk of complications from the pill is much lower than the complications from pregnancy (Edlow, MD, MSc and Bartz, MD, MPH, 2010). To avoid these more serious risks, progestin-only pills may be preferred.

Tips

Additionally, side effects can be more drastic if the pill is not taken at a consistent time. The pill is designed to keep hormone levels at a consistent level. If the body tries to deviate from these levels, then more severe side effects can be experienced. Fortunately, after a few months of initial acclimation to a new drug, the body learns how to cope. Often women experience increased satisfaction as their side effects subside after several months (Mona et al., 2021).

Regardless of the experienced side effects, another positive aspect of this method is the ease with which it can be discontinued. If the user is dissatisfied with their side effects, then switching to another is simple. A doctor can consult on the situation and counsel the patient as needed. The doctor may discuss the time it takes to switch from one pill (or method) to another. A new contraceptive may need time to start its effects, and additional methods, like barrier methods, may be advised during the transition.

Although the body needs time to regulate hormone levels, the pill's effects are reversible.

CONSIDERATIONS

Progestin-only pills are the preferred treatment method for those suffering from health concerns like endometriosis since their short-term pathway tends to reduce bleeding, painful cramps, and other negative premenstrual syndrome (PMS) symptoms (Weisburg and Fraser, 2015). According to another systematic review, combo pills can also help reduce painful periods after six months of use (Wong et al., 2009).

In general, certain risk factors may put a user at a higher likelihood of adverse effects, and therefore hormonal birth control prescription is not permitted (Mona et al., 2021). These include, but are not limited to, people who:

• Are older than thirty-five and smoke
• Have a history of breast cancer

- Have a history of high blood pressure
- Have a history of heart attacks or heart disease
- Have a history of stroke
- Have a history of blood clotting disorders
- Have had diabetes for more than ten years
- Have had a history of depression or PMDD

Another important consideration for this type of birth control is access. I have heard repeated stories of troubling access interruptions (e.g., insurance coverage gaps, work schedule irregularity, commute changes) causing women distress and inability to get their pills. If access to care might change in the near future or if it would be detrimental to health if the pill was unavailable for a time, it might be worthwhile to consider a long-acting method.

Depending on a person's specific medical plan, each pill pack may come with its own copay, leading to a regular expense to account for. Certain pill packs can come with a several-month supply, which could be particularly advantageous for individuals who can't make it during normal pharmacy hours on a monthly basis. Some pharmacies can also mail these medications depending on state regulations.

Communicating preexisting medical conditions, family medical history, and lifestyle schedule with a doctor will be an important part of deciding which method will work best.

Misconception: Hormonal contraceptives (e.g., the pill) affect and reduce long-term fertility.

A common worry talked about is the question of contraception affecting and reducing long-term fertility. This is not found in research. According to Girum and Wasie's 2018 systematic review and meta-analysis (highest levels of evidence-based research), ovulation-suppressing pills may even contribute to extended fertility since a female's finite egg reserve is preserved. Fertility concerns can be warranted when assessing fertility immediately after discontinuing the pill since the body needs time (typically three months) to regulate back to normal hormone levels. In other words, females may have trouble conceiving in these first three months, but after hormone levels regulate, fertility resumes as normal.

Misconception: The birth control pill causes cancer.

The controversy of the pill and cancer is quite complex and has been a heavily debated topic for years. New studies and research continually surface. In general, the birth control pill tends to be linked to a decrease in endometrial, ovarian, and colon cancer. The pill is linked to an increase in cervical cancer for those using the pill for five years or more, but the risk decreases the longer the pill is discontinued (National Cancer Institute, 2018).

The more complex conversation is between the pill and breast cancer. In studies that showed the pill was linked to an increase in breast cancer, the people studied were using high-dose estrogen combo pills. In contrast, no relation exists conclusively between low-dose estrogen combo pills and breast cancer. Those with a history of breast cancer should NOT use a hormonal contraceptive in general, as it can stimulate breast cancer growth. People with a family history of breast cancer should take that into special consideration in their conversations with their doctor in choosing a contraceptive (Breast Cancer, 2014).

PUTTING IT ALL TOGETHER

All in all, the birth control pill method is the most popular reversible contraceptive in the US since it feels familiar—it's like taking other medicines, has high effectiveness, and has decades of research proving safety and reversibility.

The main thing to consider with this method is its dependence on user consistency. Forgetting to bring the medication on a trip or accidentally snoozing a phone alarm reminder could feel like an innocent mistake yet result in unintended outcomes like uncomfortable side effects or an unplanned pregnancy.

Could Gina have found a better fit? With more research and technological advancements on the horizon, people like Gina may soon be able to determine their base hormone levels and identify genetic markers that predict which pill would best prevent harmful side effects.

I believe it is possible to thrive.

Perhaps the right fit for her has not been invented yet. Through development, we can help empower women when providing more control over their health. Right now, it is important to learn the truth about our options, determine whether any methods can currently serve us, and, if not, continue to push for society to see our needs and create the legacy we envision.

EMERGENCY CONTRACEPTION (EC)

Beverly was a senior in high school, and she was excited for her next chapter in life. Although she knew how to find answers for school projects and papers, she had a lot of unanswered life questions. She loved her parents and they loved her, but they had a superficial relationship. She never really felt like she could be fully open with them. Her friends provided support and helped fill in knowledge gaps she was missing, especially regarding birth control.

During her last year of high school, she wanted to experience more before entering college. Beverly opened herself up to dating Lukas; he was a friend who volunteered with her on weekends. They often found themselves repeatedly pairing up. Of course, Beverly would slyly try to stand next to him right before events started. When asked to pair up, she would give him the eyes that said, "Oh hey, why don't we?"

After three months of this, their friend groups naturally began intermingling. They found themselves studying together, eating out together, and attending school events together. All their friends knew Beverly and Lukas liked each other. Beverly's best friend Sarah became fed up with the two chickens and confronted Lukas in between classes, "Ask Beverly out already. We both know she's going to say yes."

Finally, after their friend group finished a game night celebrating the end of fall semester, Lukas mustered up the courage to ask, "Are you going home right away? Wanna get some dessert?"

Beverly's heart and stomach fluttered. "Sure!" she replied.

Their friends all approved of this match, seeing how happy they were, and after a few months, the young couple spent more free time alone and gradually started getting more intimate. Beverly and Lukas agreed they both wanted to be more physical with each other. Ideally, they would end up in colleges close to each other after graduation, but they had different life goals and agreed they wouldn't compromise their life plans for this relationship. They agreed they could be lifelong friends regardless of how things panned out, and it was settled; they were set on a short-term, exploratory relationship.

Beverly had never had sex before, but she trusted Lukas. She was aware Lukas had had sex before but was not the player type. He truly cared about Beverly, and they both mutually wanted it, so they did it.

At first, Beverly's experience was awkward and uncomfortable. Lukas was very gentle and attentive to Beverly during sex, making sure she felt comfortable and enjoyed it. Fortunately, their experience improved over time. Again, they both had future plans and did not want a pregnancy during this time, so they used male condoms and it worked well for them.

Until it didn't.

Lukas always knew to check the condoms after sex to make sure the little swimmers were all accounted for. This time, when Lukas checked the condom, he noticed something odd; he saw a rip in the condom, which meant some had clearly escaped. "But we didn't do anything differently," he said.

Beverly was stunned in outward silence and inward turmoil. She felt the weight of this responsibility fall on her, and it seemed unfair. Although they had both entered into this as a team, she was ultimately the one deciding what happened to her body next.

She knew Lukas was not at fault and she should not direct her anger at him, but he was the only one there and she took it out on him, saying, "Please get out! I need to deal with this."

He wondered if it could really be his fault and left. She regretted sending him out since now all she wanted to do was cry and find comfort in his arms. She called Sarah; she would know what to do.

Sarah freaked out and jumped onto the internet, realizing Beverly was in trouble. "Okay, there are four options for how we can do this: one, insert a copper IUD, which is 99.9 percent effective, but you need a doctor to insert it. Do you have a doctor or know a clinic that can insert it right away? Also, I'm not quite sure if they'll need to tell your parents—"

"No, my parents can't know!" Beverly panicked.

"Okay, okay, jeez. The second option is the Yuzpe method. It has a range of effectiveness. Oh wait, can't do this one because you need these specific types of birth control pills on hand. The next option is the Ella morning-after pill, but you need a prescription to get it... alright, this sounds familiar. The old-school morning-after pill is the fourth option. It works better the sooner you take it. Huh, not sure where we can find it this late, but my older sister Tracy might have more ideas about where we can get it. I'll call you right back. I'm gonna go ask her."

"Sarah, please don't leave! Can you just add her to the call?"

"Of course, babe. I just assumed you would want to be my anonymous friend."

"Ugh, that's true. I do want to be anonymous. I just won't say anything; don't mention my name!"

The dial tone connected. "Hey, Trace. My friend is in trouble. She needs the morning-after pill, but she's not sure how to get it. What can we do? ... No, not Beverly.

I can't even imagine that happening... Seriously? Your friend has some right now? The nurse on campus gave it to her? That's amazing! I'll be right over to get it. Thank you so much! See you soon, bye! Love you, too. Bye." Click. "Hello?"

"Sarah, oh my god! I can't believe her friend just has it on hand like that!"

"I know, right? I'll go pick it up and bring it to you right after, okay? Be right there."

Within twenty minutes of hanging up the phone, Sarah arrived and hugged Beverly in support. She pulled out a box from her purse and passed it to Beverly. "My sister mentioned it would still be a good idea to take a pregnancy test, just in case you don't get your period in the next three weeks."

HOW IT WORKS

MORNING-AFTER PILLS

Beverly's story was inspired by a young person's video blog from the Bedsider article, "Emergency contraception: the back-up plan." This story teaches us many important things about emergency contraception (EC). Starting with Sarah's quick internet search, she was right in finding several available EC methods. We will start by identifying the two major types of morning-after pills:

- Progestin-based pills
- Ulipristal-based pills

Progestin-Based Pills

The more common morning-after pills, shown often in the media, are ones like Plan B or Next Choice. These contain a high dose of progestin that can immediately prevent egg release (ovulation) after unprotected sex or contraceptive misuse. Therefore, if sperm is present but an egg is not present, no pregnancy can occur.

What happens if the egg ovulates right before progestin-based EC is taken? The egg could have already been present, and sperm could have found its way to the egg. Progestin-based pills would then have no true effect on pregnancy prevention (Gemzell-Danielsson, 2010). However, progestin-based pills usually have a good chance of working since ovulated eggs only survive for twenty-four hours. This method, as Beverly and Sarah found, may be more readily available at a moment's notice.

Ulipristal-Based Pills

Ella is currently the only morning-after ulipristal-based pill on the market. Ulipristal blocks the body's natural progesterone, also preventing egg release but through a different biochemical pathway (PPFA, 2022).

What happens if the egg ovulates right before Ella is taken? Some research suggests ulipristal may negatively affect sperm function. Also, it may slow down the movement of an egg in the fallopian tubes. This may help, as sperm may be unable to reach the egg if it is too deep in the fallopian tubes, and the egg may not survive by the time it does reach sperm. Therefore, Ella may still be effective even if a person suspects they may have ovulated recently (Rosato et al., 2016).

<u>Morning-After Pill Considerations and Tips</u>
Progestin-based morning-after pills can be used up to five days after an emergency incident. The five-day time frame comes from how long sperm survive within the female reproductive system. However, the more time that passes, the less effective progestin-based pills are, especially after day three.

Ella has been shown to be more effective than progestin-based pills. It is marketed to have the same level of effectiveness within a full five-day span. If an Ella prescription can be requested and received within five days after an emergency incident, it may be a more effective option than progestin-based pills.

Importantly, progestin and ulipristal can interfere with one another in the short term. Progestin methods *increase* progestin to delay ovulation and thicken cervical mucus. Ella works to *decrease* the body's progesterone, delaying ovulation until sperm die after five days. After taking Ella, it is generally recommended to wait about five days until starting a new, regular hormonal contraceptive since progestin is typically present. Lastly, if another moment requiring EC occurs again within five days of first use, it is recommended to take the same exact morning-after pill again to avoid possible interference (PPFA, 2022).

YUZPE METHOD

If a person already uses the pill for contraception, an EC method to consider might be the Yuzpe method. Depending on the specific pill already prescribed, users could potentially increase the dosages in a shortened amount of time to abruptly prevent ovulation in an emergency situation. It is worth knowing this method exists, but as for the exact regimen, the best person to consult is the prescribing doctor. When selecting a contraceptive pill, this may be a valuable consideration since users would have these pills immediately available in an emergency (Bedsider, 2010).

THE COPPER IUD

The copper IUD can be placed as EC up to five days after an emergency incident. It is a non-hormonal EC and works by releasing copper ions that effectively prevent pregnancy. (More on this in the Copper IUD chapter.) The drawback is it must be placed by a medical provider, and the patient has to quickly schedule an appointment when the clock is already ticking.

EFFECTIVENESS

The effectiveness of all these methods depends on implementing the method within five days of sperm presence in the female reproductive system.

MORNING-AFTER PILLS
Progestin-Based Pills

Although no method offers 100 percent effectiveness (aside from abstinence), Beverly was fortunately able to take this form of EC within a few hours of her emergency. Her chance of pregnancy dropped from 87 percent to about 25 percent. For others taking it later than this, effectiveness may be further reduced (PPFA, 2022).

Ulipristal-Based Pills
With Ella, the chance of being pregnant drops from 87 percent to about 15 percent (PPFA, 2022).

YUZPE METHOD
This method has a range of effectiveness depending on the specific type of pill used, dropping the chances of pregnancy from 87 percent to about 15 to 44 percent (Bosworth, MD et al., 2014).

THE COPPER IUD
The most effective emergency contraception, at 99.9 percent effectiveness, is the copper IUD (Bedsider, 2019).

BMI AND EFFECTIVENESS
When a person has a high BMI, EC effectiveness may vary.

Progestin-based morning-after pills work well for those under 155 pounds, and Ella is effective for those who are up to 195 pounds. For those with weights beyond that, the copper IUD becomes the best choice. Part of the reason the copper IUD is so effective is its predictable effectiveness on people regardless of BMI (PPFA, 2022). An added benefit of the copper IUD as EC is it can be left in as a long-term contraceptive method, providing protection from future emergency situations.

STI PROTECTION

No emergency contraceptive provides protection against STIs. In an emergency, a healthcare provider can be sought out to perform tests and check for any STI onset.

SIDE EFFECTS

Some lightheadedness, tender breasts, and nausea can occur around the time an EC morning-after pill is taken. Less commonly, intense nausea can be experienced since these pills contain a high dosage of hormones to initiate their effects. Some people get an upset stomach and throw up the pills. If that happens within two hours of taking the EC pill, they will not work. After letting the nausea run its course, the person would need to take an EC pill again.

Additionally, period changes during the next menstrual cycle may occur. Painful cramps increase or decrease bleeding during menses, and even spotting between periods can be expected after taking these pills. Of course, a doctor should be consulted if users have any health concerns. However, these are common (and sadly uncomfortable) side effects (PPFA, 2022).

CONSIDERATIONS

Since timing is a major concern with ECs, healthcare professionals may offer to provide some of these pills to a patient for future unforeseen circumstances. Tracy's friend had them on hand for this reason. She felt confident that if her primary mode of contraception was mishandled or forgotten, she had a backup method prepared. Nevertheless, a consideration for providers is establishing trust. Many patients may feel sensitive about their lifestyles, and premature judgment may be poorly received.

For added benefit, these medications can even be shipped directly to a person's doorstep.

Morning-after pill ECs can range from twenty to seventy dollars, and access varies depending on state laws and regulations. These costs can be partially or fully covered with insurance or government funding. Many family planning clinics can have these on-site, and they can be called in advance to see what assistance they can provide. If they cannot give it for free, perhaps they can help find ways to attain it while keeping financial and anonymity constraints in mind. Depending on the state, they may or may not be able to dispense ECs and/or honor the privacy concerns of minors. In certain states, pharmacies carry the progestin-based methods, and people usually can request these EC pills from the pharmacist without showing an ID or disclosing age (see the Resources section for some helpful information).

COMMON MISCONCEPTIONS

Misconception: The more a person uses EC morning-after pills, the less effective they become over time.

A worry that comes up often is EC pills will not work as well the more they are used. San Francisco comedian Ali Wong joked in her comedy special on Netflix, "Baby Cobra," how she used to take Plan B "like Skittles." Although EC pills should not be taken by the "handful," they can be used repeatedly without impacting the effectiveness of future EC pill use. Also, these pills do not affect overall health in the long term (Vandergriendt, Goldman, Nwadike, MD, MPH, 2020).

It is important to remember that the range of effectiveness does vary tremendously, and timing is a huge factor since sperm can live for a relatively long time. Relying on this as a primary method of contraception is not recommended. We have and will discuss more effective, reliable methods in this book.

Misconception: Taking multiple morning-after pills at once increases effectiveness.

Taking multiple doses of Ella or Plan B at once does *not* make it more effective. This does not work, and it can make a person overly nauseous and throw up the pills, leaving them useless.

Misconception: Morning-after EC pills are abortion pills.

The morning-after pill is *not* the same as the abortion pill. The start of pregnancy is legally and biologically defined as the time the embryo (united sperm and egg) embed into the wall of the uterus. EC methods, as we have covered, block egg release.

Some people misconceive EC pills as abortion pills. However, abortion pills stop a developing embryo *after* it embeds in the uterus, whereas EC pills prevent them from embedding in the first place. This is the goal of all other contraceptives, too. With EC pills, no embryo has been formed to abort.

PUTTING IT ALL TOGETHER

Emergency contraception is a fallback emergency method, not a primary method. ECs can be kept on hand in case of emergencies since unplanned scenarios can arise in people's (and their friend's) lives. ECs are safe to use when used as directed, but some temporary changes in periods can occur as well as nausea. If a drug store is too difficult to get to, often family planning clinics have them stocked, and they can be called for additional guidance and resources.

Lastly, for some, the shame barrier can be one of the hardest to overcome. Some people may be afraid or find it embarrassing to ask for emergency contraception, and it may cause them not to seek it out at all. Accidents happen, and millions of people (and millions more that have not reported it) have taken these pills.

Involving a partner, family members, and friends, if it feels safe doing so, can be a huge support. When fears and emotions are elevated, a support network, whoever that may be, can help.

BARRIER METHODS

Layana always knew what to say. She got along easily with people and worked in a stable job doing administrative work for the local government. One of her many passions was makeup; she enjoyed designing and producing her own eye-shadow palettes.

Layana had her five- and ten-year plans in motion: get her favorite R&B artist to endorse her products and get into a major makeup distribution company. At this time, she and her boyfriend Kevin had a five-year-old daughter named Sasha. They both wanted to grow their family in the next few years, but Layana wanted to focus on her career goals before having another child.

She and Kevin initially had no problems using condoms, but sometimes, in the heat of the moment they would not use condoms at the beginning of intercourse. Layana decided to use the pill since she had heard of people getting pregnant from pre-ejaculate.

Layana had a difficult time adjusting to the birth control pill. She had a rare reaction where she was nauseous most mornings and her breasts were overly tender to the point where her arms radiated pain during her period (Bass, 2022). Her doctor suggested she stop using the pill and instead use a condom with a diaphragm, sponge, or cervical cap as an extra precaution. She liked this idea since it did not solely rely on putting on a condom immediately before sex.

Layana asked her doctor for the Caya (SILCS) diaphragm prescription since the sponge was single-use and she was tired of paying for condoms regularly. The other diaphragm (the Milex) and the cervical cap required finding the right size, and she did not want to spend time finding a fit (CooperSurgical, 2022).

Her doctor prescribed her the Caya and dispensed a tube of spermicide to use with it. She thought the diaphragm almost looked like a miniature trampoline with a reinforced rim encircling a flexible surface, although the center portion was shaped like a bowl.

At first, things were messy. Layana was instructed to place spermicide into the bowl of the diaphragm. When she was ready to place it in her vagina, she pinched together its reinforced rim and squeezed it a little too forcefully, getting the spermicide all over herself when she was supposed to let it sit mostly within the cup. It was not the most comfortable thing to do, but she got it into place in front of her cervix, and once she let go, it felt fine. Now she was ready for a test run.

Kevin came home a few hours later, and after Sasha had dinner and went to bed, Layana excitedly led Kevin to their bedroom. He was surprised at what had gotten into Layana (she planned to tell him after) but did not question it. He put on a condom and happily went to bed with her.

"How was that?" Layana asked when they were both relaxed in each other's arms.

"Super hot," he replied as he started to doze off.

She playfully nudged him, "But how did it feel?"

"Really good, babe, you're amazing..." He drifted off to sleep.

Layana relished in the moment of feeling safe and comfortable with her new layer of protection as she peacefully went to sleep.

***

When Layana later told Kevin about her diaphragm, he did feel like he wished he could have been more involved in the decision and almost felt worried she was trying to hide it from him. When she revealed she only wanted to test if they could feel it, he felt better knowing she trusted their communication and openness. After a while, he would even help her insert it and remove it if she needed assistance.

Layana and Kevin's story is a fictional composite inspired by real peoples' contraception journeys. They and many others openly share reviews of all methods on bedsider. org, which can help put unfamiliar methods into a more approachable lens.

HOW IT WORKS

Layana's doctor presented her with four non-hormonal barrier method options that would help put contraceptive control in her hands:

- The diaphragm
- The sponge
- The cervical cap
- The female (or internal) condom

The first three methods on this list are fully inserted within a female's vaginal canal covering the cervix. They serve to block sperm from traveling to (or beyond) the cervix. These first three methods all need spermicide to be most effective, as sperm can swim around these devices if they are not positioned perfectly. Spermicide helps to further seal the entrance to the cervix and affects sperm's swimming ability. Spermicide must contact sperm for six hours to work. In other words, these devices (and the surrounding spermicide) must be left in the vagina for six hours after sex.

While male condoms are typically referred to as *condoms*, female (internal) condoms are also available on the market. The fourth method on the list, although called an *internal* condom, is important to note since part of it remains outside of the vagina externally.

The diaphragm is a reusable, cupped, two-inch silicone device. As Layana noted, the diaphragm has a rounded portion where spermicide sits. It has an outer rim that flexes and allows the user to squeeze it to fit into the vaginal canal and cover the cervix. The spermicide end of the cup should be facing the cervix. To remove, the user hooks their finger onto the diaphragm rim and pulls it out. This method needs a prescription and comes in various sizes. It can be placed up to eighteen hours before sex (Bedsider, 2019).

The sponge is a one-time use, over-the-counter device made of plastic foam. It has a dimple on one side, which is placed in front of the cervix, and it has a nylon loop across the opposite end to help with removal. The sponge has spermicide within it that gets activated when gently squeezed. It is available without a prescription in drug stores (even online) and can be placed up to twenty-four hours before sex (Bedsider, 2019).

The cervical cap is made of silicone and is reusable (typically for two years). It has several components. It looks like a cough syrup measuring cup with shallow walls, a wide-rimmed opening, and rather than a flat base, an indented dome with a narrow-rimmed opening. A loop runs across the cup's opening for convenient placement and retrieval (MFMER, 2022). Both ends of the cup are reservoirs for spermicide. Sometimes air gets trapped behind the cap, and it can be difficult to remove at first.

Pushing it in a little before fully removing it may help relieve some of the suction pressure. This method also requires a prescription and can be placed six hours before sex (PPFA, 2022).

<u>Internal condoms</u> come in individual wrappers. They are soft and flexible nitrile tubes with a closed end and an open end. Both ends have a reinforced ring. The closed end has a thicker ring, which is inserted into the vagina and placed near the cervix. The open end has a thinner ring that trails out of the vagina. The outer ring helps this end stay outside of the vaginal canal. During vaginal sex, a penis would enter through the outer ring into the internal condom, staying within the covered vaginal canal. Similarly, internal condoms can also be used for anal sex. Internal condoms can be purchased in convenience stores or online. If planning ahead, internal condoms can be placed up to two hours ahead of time (CDC, 2022).

Additionally, only one male barrier method currently exists, the male (external) condom.

<u>External condoms</u> are flexible tubes that come in different sizes, usually made of latex. They are rolled up and individually packed. External condoms trap sperm within the tube so sperm does not enter the female reproductive system. Some condoms have spermicide and/or lubrication already on them, and different brands can be compared for comfort. Male condoms can be purchased in stores or online. Many health clinics leave them out for free, no questions asked (Bedsider, 2019). When putting one on, the proper orientation needs to be determined so it can

unroll easily. If it does not unroll, then it may be on the wrong way and need to be flipped. External condoms are typically placed on right before sex since the penis needs to be erect for the condom to stay in place.

EFFECTIVENESS

Overall, the sponge, cervical cap, and diaphragm with spermicide are not as effective as many other methods discussed in this book. Their range is anywhere from 70–86 percent effective with typical use. However, these can be used with either a male or female condom to increase overall effectiveness (Bedsider, 2019).

In theory, both types of condoms can be over 90 percent effective with perfect use, but the reality is, as some stories go, they break. Typical use is about 79–82 percent effective. All condom material is temperature- and humidity-sensitive. Appropriate storage and shipping environment cannot be guaranteed. For instance, condoms taken out of wallets should not be trusted, as they may be unknowingly damaged by friction or possibly even expired (Bedsider, 2019).

External condoms and internal condoms are our most effective contraceptive methods for preventing sexually transmitted infections (STIs). In contrast to the other barrier methods, both types of condoms protect the entirety of the mouth, penis, vagina, and/or anus since they fully encircle these body parts. External condoms and internal condoms should be used when a bed partner is not monogamous, i.e., either person has multiple partners or if a sex partner's STI status is unknown. STIs each tend to come with their own set of harm. Some can have serious and permanent effects on health. We can try to avoid and protect ourselves from these harms with condom barriers (OASH, 2019).

When attempting to prevent both STIs and pregnancy, condoms and other non-barrier birth control methods can be used together. The most effective combination for preventing STIs and pregnancy would be both a condom (internal or external) and a long-acting reversible contraceptive (we will cover these later) (OASH, 2019).

SIDE EFFECTS

Appropriately, Layana left the diaphragm in after sex. For optimal effectiveness, these methods should be left in for at least six hours after sex to ensure the sperm has enough contact time with the spermicide. However, they should not be left in too long either since they can start to accumulate bacteria. The sponge must be removed after thirty hours total, the cervical cap forty-eight hours total, and the diaphragm twenty-four hours total. These methods can tamper with the delicate pH of the vagina if left in too long, creating yeast or bacterial infections (Bedsider, 2019).

A person can experience sensitivity or allergy to barrier method materials, spermicides, and/or lubricants. Furthermore, some people become more prone to UTIs with these methods since spermicides or lubricants can get messy.

People who are allergic to latex often feel at a loss since they can't use certain condoms comfortably. Non-latex male condoms are available in stores and online and can be made of synthetic or natural materials. An effective alternative can be female condoms since they are usually made of nitrile (Bedsider, 2019).

Make sure to listen to the body and reflect if something does not feel right. Providing feedback and evaluating helps both partners enjoy experiences fully.

CONSIDERATIONS

The cervical cap and the diaphragm can be rinsed and stored to use again. They can last years but continually need to be evaluated for holes or damage. This reusability can be financially advantageous for some people.

Male and female condoms can gradually slip out of position during sex and get pushed into the vagina or anus. Both partners can have difficulty sensing this. Periodically checking the condom's position may be necessary.

Latex condoms are prone to breaking when using oil-based lubes. Using oil-based lubes with condoms is not advised. If a condom breaks, it would be a good idea to consider emergency contraception like Plan B or Ella (as we discussed previously).

Sponges, cervical caps, diaphragms, and internal condoms are powerful contraceptive tools, as they can be controlled by people with a uterus. Some people have trouble remembering to put on a male condom right before sex. Some people prefer not to use a male condom, as they may not enjoy how it feels. The other barrier methods can provide protection and may be more comfortable.

Once inserted properly, females using these methods do not typically feel or notice them. If it feels uncomfortable, it may not be in the correct position; likely, it is not deep enough. It should be about finger-length away from the vaginal opening and fully cover the cervix (CDC, 2022).

To Layana's contentment, Kevin couldn't detect her diaphragm during sex, and they can use this method in addition to a male (or female) condom for more peace of mind. Other times, partners can detect a difference and may or may not prefer the feeling.

Either way, the best outcomes stem from clear communication and collaborating on expectations.

COMMON MISCONCEPTIONS
Misconception: People cannot become pregnant from pre-ejaculate.

Sperm is present in a high enough concentration in pre-ejaculate alone to achieve pregnancy. The male condom must be flipped to the right orientation before placement. If the male condom touches the head of the penis with the incorrect side, ensure no pre-ejaculate gets onto the external surface since sperm *is* present in pre-ejaculate and can lead to pregnancy. When in doubt, the male condom should be discarded and replaced with a new one.

Misconception: Using two condoms, e.g., one male and one female condom OR two male condoms OR two female condoms, provides even more protection.

Only one condom, either a female or male condom, should be used at a time. If any two are used at once, it creates additional friction and both are more likely to break. Instead, either a female or male condom can be used with a diaphragm, sponge, or cervical cap. Alternatively, to increase protection, one barrier method plus an additional non-barrier method can be used together (CDC, 2022).

Misconception: Condoms are reusable.

Condoms are not reusable. Even with careful handling, once removed, sperm and bacteria can spill out to other surfaces of the condom, which can then be transferred to a partner. Once used and left out, condoms can be prone to breaking since they have already been stretched out and likely dried out.

Misconception: Barrier methods are as effective as withdrawal and fertility-based awareness methods.

According to the Office on Women's Health (a branch of the US Department of Health and Human Services), the diaphragm and the sponge are considered more effective than withdrawal and fertility-based awareness methods with typical use.

<u>Withdrawal</u> is when the penis is removed from the vagina or anus or mouth before ejaculation, or "pulling out." Special care must be taken so no pre-ejaculation enters their partner either.

<u>Fertility-based awareness</u> is a type of method where people do not have sex the days an egg is present in the female reproductive system. When an egg is not present in the female reproductive system, even if sperm is present, pregnancy cannot occur. Pregnancy requires both sperm and egg. Several ways exist for females to track their egg release days (ovulation), such as tracking period cycle days, checking cervical mucus consistency/color, taking body temperature, and breastfeeding (Bedsider, 2019). (Additional information can be found in the Resources section.)

Withdrawal and fertility-based awareness methods can work well for some people and typically have no side effects. Some people highly prefer these more natural methods for this reason. However, they do require self-awareness and discipline. Withdrawal and fertility-based awareness methods can be simultaneously used with barrier methods to increase overall effectiveness and protect against STIs.

The sponge, diaphragm, and cervical cap can beneficially give females some contraceptive control. This could be especially helpful before a night out when it might be difficult to remember if or when a male condom was used. For maximum effectiveness, spermicide is needed for these methods. Again, these methods are definitely prone to accidents and are on the lower end of reliability. For those averse to hormonal method side effects, those without access to other methods, those that want an extra backup method (e.g., they forgot their routine birth control method), and those that may be open to having children if all else goes awry, these methods can be good options, especially in conjunction with condoms.

Good quality internal and external condoms can be reliable methods that help prevent pregnancy and STIs if used correctly and consistently. Both partners in a sexual relationship can communicate their contraception preferences and collaborate to keep each other comfortable and safe.

THE PATCH AND THE RING

Vera was from Fort Worth, Texas, a small city west of Dallas. Over one thousand miles from home at New York University (the university of her dreams), she reflected on her last few months of family time. She fondly pictured her sisters and mom all watching their favorite true crime shows with her.

Vera's entire family was extremely proud of her for being the first one to go to college. She wanted to make a name for herself and live up to her family's expectations. As she soaked in the excitement of this new adventure, she brushed off her mild twinge of homesickness and honed in on her excitement to study criminology.

Vera's new roommate barged in with three full-sized suitcases and her familial posse carrying an array of approved living items. "Ah! You must be Vera!" she screamed as she went in for an overly familiar embrace. Vera peeled back from her view of the assertive young woman's brunette hair to get her greeting in.

"And you must be Zoey! Do you need any help unpacking? Feel free to move things around."

"No need. We helped my older siblings move to college years ago, and now my family's got this down to a science. But we're going to get dinner after if you want to join?" Before Vera could respond, Zoey then whispered, "And I overheard some other students saying there's a big party tonight near one of the other dorms. Wanna come with me?"

Vera was torn between fears of going to her first college party and of offending her new roommate. So she sided with pushing herself to make friends. "Sure!" she said.

After dinner, the freshmen girls parted from Zoey's family and went to gather with other students in the common space area, going through the exciting pleasantries of meeting an influx of new potential friends. One way or another, word got around and it seemed like most people were going to attend this party Zoey had mentioned. About an hour before they were about to leave, Zoey brought Vera back to their room so they could get ready together.

The two of them looked through their wardrobes and consulted each other on what kind of "vibe" they should go for. As Zoey applied her makeup in her vanity mirror, her phone alarm went off. She abruptly put down her brush, rummaged through her drawers, and pulled out a pack of pills.

Vera could not help but stare at her roommate's sudden movements.

"I know, it feels like a weird time to take it, but I'm from the west coast and normally, I'd take it after dinner."

"Sorry, take what?"

"Oh, my birth control. Are you on the pill or something else? I've been wanting to try something else since I've been single for the last year, and I haven't been consistent with taking it every day. Our schedules are about to go crazy, so I know I won't be able to take it. I'm very forgetful. I think our school health center has resources, so I'll check that out at some point." Zoey went back to applying her makeup and did not pry into Vera's contemplative silence.

Vera's conservative upbringing provided no knowledge of birth control, and she realized she wanted to know more. Her mom and dad had her at a very young age, and although she adored her parents for the life they gave her, she felt they only had time for her and their busy work schedules. Vera wanted to have children after graduating college and after she had the chance to travel out of the country.

In the middle of her first week of classes, Vera stared at her newly organized calendar, stupefied at the sight of quizzes, tests, and paper due dates. She started feeling a bit overwhelmed and decided to take a walk through campus to clear her mind. A campus map was right outside her dorm, and she scanned it. She realized she was near the school's health center. Vera's curiosity returned as she remembered her birth control conversation with Zoey, and she walked to the building.

Outside the health center, a small poster caught her attention, showing how students could sign up for health visits online, including visits concerning women's health. She searched on her phone, saw she had coverage under her school's insurance plan, and scheduled an appointment right after her next class.

At her appointment, after Vera filled out some medical forms, Mary, the nurse practitioner, called her in. Vera thought she seemed like such a jolly lady; she had a confident smile and a booming sense of humor. They walked together into a small clinic room. It had a patient chair with a disposable paper lining, a computer, cabinets and counters with various boxes and jars of medical supplies, and a wall of paper brochures. Vera sat on the patient chair.

Vera's nurse practitioner helped her feel comfortable right away, getting to know her and giving her tips on places in New York she ought to visit when she had time. "Why don't you start by telling me what brings you in today," Mary said, "and I'm going to start by taking your vitals."

"I wanted to learn more about birth control. My roommate uses the pill, and she mentioned she doesn't like keeping on that schedule. I mean, I'm not sexually active right now and haven't been before, but I'm curious if it would make sense to learn about it now before anything comes up when I don't have the time."

Mary motioned over to a big chart on the wall. "As you can see, you have many options to choose from. But let me ask you which of these is most important to you: reliability, comfort, routine, or familiarity?"

"I'm not familiar with any option, and it doesn't necessarily have to be reliable since I'm not active... I guess routine since I have a busy schedule and don't want to worry about it interfering too much, but comfort is a close second."

"Got it! I'll send you an email with a link for all the options since I want you to review them for yourself. But to me, it sounds like the patch, the ring, or the shot might be a good match for you. They are all very effective as well, with perfect use, meaning you stick to the schedule perfectly and use it properly, but effectiveness is lower in reality."

Vera was afraid of needles. She tended to procrastinate on getting her flu shot every year and worried her fear might disrupt a shot routine. "The thought of getting a shot is already making me nervous. What's the patch like?"

"The patch is kind of like a band-aid. It releases synthetic estrogen and progesterone hormones to control your cycle and help prevent ovulation while also thickening your cervical mucus so sperm can't enter your uterus. Do you have any issues with sensitive skin or a latex allergy?"

"My skin is very sensitive, and I actually do have a latex allergy." She thought back to the times she would get a rash when doctors examined her with latex gloves. "I don't think I like the idea of having to check it all the time either. What about the ring?"

"You can think of the ring as a silicone hair tie with hormones that slowly release when introduced to your body temperature. It works similarly to the patch. You put it into your vagina yourself once a month, take it out before the week of your period, and place a new one back in after your period. Have you ever used a tampon? It kind of feels like that."

"I have. Is it possible for the ring to go too far up and get lost? Could it potentially get stuck there?"

"Don't worry, there's nowhere for it to go! This is your reproductive organs, not the Mall of America!" She laughed boisterously at her own joke, and Vera contagiously joined in.

She liked the sound of this option and expressed she wanted to do some more research on it. Mary agreed with her choice and quickly left the room and came back holding a thin foil package. "Here, I'll give you a NuvaRing sample to try out as well."

After leaving Health Services, Vera was free for the rest of the afternoon, and she knew Zoey was going to be in class for the next few hours. She searched the different methods on the internet and felt she agreed with Mary about the ring, although she wished she was a good candidate for the patch. She noted the main difficulty people had with this method was their partners could sometimes feel it during sex (not a problem for her right now), and insertion and removal could be difficult. She watched some how-to videos and felt she was up for the challenge.

Taking the sample NuvaRing Mary had given her, Vera decided to give it a go. She fumbled around for a good twenty minutes but finally got it in. At first, it kept inching its way out and felt uncomfortable, but she realized she had to fit it farther up. Once it was in the right place, she could not feel it at all. She practiced retrieving it and was able to loop her finger through the ring and pull it back down. *This was way easier than putting it in,* she thought. After a positive first month on this method, she contacted Mary to get a prescription and started this new college journey feeling confident, excited, and grateful.

***

Vera's story was inspired by Katie White's video blog review on YouTube called "My Birth Control Experience Experience: NuvaRing vs. Pill | NuvaRing review, side effects and how to use." Many people like Katie and Vera use the ring routinely for contraception and find success with it after they surpass the learning curve.

HOW IT WORKS

Although the patch and the ring are different methods, they work fairly similarly. We will compare them side-by-side in each of our discussions.

THE PATCH

As Mary explained to Vera, the patch is applied like a Band-Aid. It is a square with 1.75-inch sides. To use it, remove it from its package and stick it to a convenient part of the body (maybe the upper arm, a butt cheek, or belly). Hormones can then pass from the patch through the skin barrier and act on the female reproductive system (PPFA, "Birth Control Patch," 2022).

One patch is worn for an entire week then switched to a new one. In the fourth week of every month, no patch is worn. During the patch weeks, users must check to make sure it is completely pressed down. If it is even partially off, the patch must be replaced (Galzote et al., 2017).

Two forms of the patch are on the market now, Xulane and Twirla. Ortho Evra was a discontinued name brand with the same hormone composition as Xulane. As with all other methods with estrogen we have discussed, risks include blood clots. The patch exposes patients to a relatively high dose of estrogen. Ortho Evra was given a black box warning and discontinued possibly over these blood clot incidents. Although the data we have currently shows the risk of blood clots is higher on the pill, the overall risk of blood clots on either method is still very low (Galzote et al., 2017).

THE RING

Two contraceptive rings are currently on the market, NuvaRing and Annovera. As Vera experienced, each NuvaRing is discarded and replaced with a new one every month, whereas a single Annovera ring can be used for an entire year. The process of using Annovera is otherwise the same. Each month, it is removed during one non-ring week, rinsed, stored, and placed back in at the end of the week (Bedsider, "Birth control ring," 2019).

Patients must also handle rings properly when they are outside the body, keeping them out of the sun and storing them in a safe place. Some people like having several NuvaRing dispensed at once to save them trips to the pharmacy or clinic. In this case, users can store their non-used NuvaRings in the fridge if planning to use them after four months or later.

Positives of this method are low progestin dose, ease of discontinuation, and once-a-month insertion. Another major benefit includes the ability to prolong and control periods. People report more regularity of their periods on the ring than on the pill due to the low amount of progestin it contains. Also, they report more satisfaction with period control (Roumen, 2008). Theoretically, if the yearly Annovera ring is left in the entire time, thirteen period cycles could be skipped safely. The NuvaRing similarly allows period control if the non-ring week is skipped and a new ring is placed right away (Bedsider, "Birth control ring," 2019).

THE PATCH

Effectiveness highly depends on how well the patch stays on a person's body. In ideal situations, perfect use is 99.7 percent effective. Various life situations can interrupt patch wear, e.g., the patch loses stickiness and falls off unnoticed, or the patch is not changed weekly. In these cases, typical use drops to 93 percent effective. All things considered, the patch ends up being as effective as the pill (Bedsider, "Birth control patch," 2019).

THE RING

While both rings differ slightly in effectiveness with perfect use—Annovera 97.3 percent and NuvaRing 99.7 percent—they end up being very similar in typical use effectiveness at 91–93 percent. Their typical use effectiveness is similar to the birth control pill.

Effectiveness drops if the ring is removed during the three active hormone weeks. If Annovera is left out for over two hours, or if NuvaRing is left out for forty-eight hours, then the ring may not provide effective contraception and users may need to use a backup method. Also, effectiveness significantly drops after five weeks of using a single NuvaRing and after one year of using a single Annovera. After this allotted time, hormones are depleted and effectiveness is no longer guaranteed (Bedsider, "Birth control ring," 2019).

Neither the patch nor the ring provides protection against STIs.

SIDE EFFECTS

THE PATCH

The main difference patients experience on the patch, compared to other hormonal contraceptives, is a heightened breast soreness for the first few weeks. Most people report the soreness resolves after a few months. The other side effects are the same ones associated with other hormonal contraceptives, such as headaches, nausea, and period changes (PPFA, "Birth Control Patch," 2022).

THE RING

Like other progestin methods, this method can affect libido (sex drive). However, the ring is reported to increase vaginal wetness and increase libido, whereas most other progestin methods tend to decrease sex drive (Roumen, 2008).

CONSIDERATIONS

THE PATCH

The patch can be a good option for those without latex issues. The main issue is about one in five people experience skin irritation. Sometimes the adhesive does not work well for their lifestyle, perhaps if they exercise frequently and sweat often. Some helpful tips for this method include placing subsequent patches onto different areas of the body in order to allow the previous area to gain relief as well as avoiding lotions or oils in those areas to prevent loosening the grip (Galzote et al., 2017).

THE RING

The main complaints around this method start with a high initial learning curve, just like placing a tampon for the first time. Those plungers are tricky! Fortunately, Vera found ways to educate herself on the ring, talked to her healthcare provider, and persistently practiced her insertion and removal technique. However, many people report struggling with finding the right insertion technique and proper place to leave it, especially if they may not be as familiar with their bodies. They may find it uncomfortable or that it falls out at first, but that is usually due to shallow placement. Removal tends to be simpler.

Additionally, people using this method might be dissatisfied by partner "inconvenience during intercourse." In Guida et al.'s 2005 study of seventy-six women, roughly 30 percent of partners felt the ring during sex, while only 11 percent of the users felt it. Satisfaction increases on this method for both the ring user and their partner when a dialogue about the expectations of the method occurs in advance. Even with these challenges, people using this method report high satisfaction.

Misconception: The patch is not as effective as the birth control pill.

Some people feel the patch is not as effective as the pill, possibly since not many other medications are regularly administered in a patch form. However, the patch's hormones readily absorb through the skin, and effectiveness is quite dependable.

Misconception: Since the ring can be left in longer, it more likely leads to infections.

The ring does not increase someone's susceptibility to infection since the ring's material is biocompatible and microflora (natural body bacteria) are not affected significantly (Huang et al., 2015).

PUTTING IT ALL TOGETHER

When used perfectly, both the patch and the ring are highly effective at preventing pregnancy. The patch is a simple method, but users must be attentive to its adhesion. While the ring requires body familiarity and practice, it does not require as much frequent maintenance. However, if the patch or ring comes off unexpectedly or is not replaced in time, effectiveness decreases and a backup method should be used.

Both methods require a prescription, which might be difficult without access to a medical provider. Nowadays, these methods can be shipped depending on individual state laws. (For more information on this, check out the Resources section or contact a healthcare provider or local health clinic.) Overall, these are both great methods that fit well into many peoples' routines.

THE SHOT

Deb was shocked. She skydived for fun, so it was almost comical that she broke her hip tripping down a few stairs in her own house; it just didn't seem hip-breaking worthy. Deb looked around the emergency room, watching patients check in and staff members attend to their duties. After her X-rays were taken and tests were performed, she reflected on the experience, and her thoughts wandered as she was doped up on pain medications. Finally, she set her gaze on the creased blanket folds atop her body, where her torso branched to her legs.

Deb's doctor, Dr. Sahin, knocked on her door, coming back to explain that the tests showed her bones had lost density. He diagnosed her with early onset osteoporosis. Deb's bones were so brittle that she had broken her hip at the age of twenty. It was strange.

We hear about seventy-, eighty-, and ninety-year-olds breaking their hips, and it is terrible. It is a sign of a severe loss of bone density since hips have the largest mass of bone in the body (NIH, 2018). This usually happens as a chronic problem over time, so for this to happen at twenty years old, Deb was dazed in her perplexity.

Initially, the doctor was surprised at this, too. He had to take a step back and think about her medical history. No one in her family had any kind of fragile bone syndrome that Deb was aware of, and she reported not having any medical conditions. Deb also claimed she had a fairly balanced diet. She was not taking any supplements, but she had been on birth control for the last three years.

Dr. Sahin pulled up research articles on the only thing listed on her medical history forms: Depo-Provera.

He knew Depo-Provera (DMPA), or "the shot," was an injectable form of contraception. Scrolling through the articles, Dr. Sahin discovered details regarding some of DMPA's side effects. Bleeding between periods and even missed periods were experienced. Changes in mood, sore breasts, and headaches could also occur, similar to the other hormonal contraception methods. Unique to Depo-Provera though is a risk of bone loss after long-term use.

A-ha! He thought. Although he felt very empathetic this had happened to her, Dr. Sahin was pleased to find that the research showed Deb's ailment was predictably reversible. If she was open to switching methods and discontinuing the shots, her bone density would return to a more normal level after about sixty weeks (Renner, 2010).

The doctor returned to Deb and relayed the news. She had a mix of emotions. Of course, she was overjoyed the mystery was solved, but she was bewildered. She did not realize this was a risk.

When Deb initially chose this method, she no longer suffered from her painful endometriosis cramps. Also, she felt the shot method was very convenient. She usually got her teeth cleaned every three months, and regularly planned these appointments on the same day, her "doctor days," she called them. The shot itself was comparable to getting the flu shot, whereas the other long-acting methods had felt a bit more involved.

Ultimately, she decided she felt content and thankful the shot served her well over the years.

***

Deb's experience was based on a friend's true story. She had used the shot for about two years, moved cities, and continued the shots through a different medical facility, using it for almost four years. She did not know what the side effects were at the time she had decided on the shot. However, now we do know how to better anticipate any severe side effects that may occur, and we will explore these together. The American College of Obstetricians and Gynecology (ACOG) and the World Health Organization (WHO) agree its positive benefits serve millions of people well (KFF, 2020).

Overall, my friend really did appreciate the convenience of this method and her alleviated endometriosis pain during the years she did use it.

HOW IT WORKS

Patients choosing the shot get a synthetic progestin injection from a healthcare provider every three months. The shot has a specific type of progestin, DMPA. DMPA was originally developed under the brand name Depo-Provera in 1959 and is one of the oldest forms of progestin we have on the market (KFF, 2020). As we now know, progestin both helps prevent egg release and thicken cervical mucus, preventing sperm from joining to an egg.

Now, an at-home version of the shot is available called SubQ Depo-Provera. This allows users to give themselves the shot every three months to increase user convenience and help ensure it is taken on time (Morse, MD, MPH, 2015). Many other drugs on the market (like insulin for diabetes) are self-administered at home successfully.

EFFECTIVENESS

When this method is administered timely and regularly, perfect use is 99.8 percent effective, while typical use is 96 percent effective. The discrepancy comes from patients missing their regularly scheduled three-month visit (Bedsider, 2019).

The shot or injectable does not provide any protection against STIs.

SIDE EFFECTS

<u>Bone Mineral Density</u>

Studies have looked back at incidents of fractures in people who have used the DMPA contraceptive shot and found they were "slightly" more likely to fracture bones the longer they used the shot compared to people who did not use the shot (Meier et al., 2010). One study found about 9.1 per one thousand people who used the DMPA contraceptive shot fractured bones, while 7.3 per one thousand people who did not use the shot also fractured bones (Lanza et al., 2013).

While these numbers only show a slight increase in risk and incidence, females with Deb's condition were unaware of the shot's effect on bone mineral density before 2004. Now, a black box warning from the FDA is printed on the brand-named Depo-Provera shot, saying the risk of bone loss may be irreversible. In reality, pregnancy health concern side effects outweigh the shot's bone health side effects since pregnancy itself can come with a negative effect on bone health too. Pregnant women need to be sure they have proper minerals and vitamins in their diet to help with their bone health since the developing baby will also need these. If not, the baby may end up absorbing their mother's natural reservoir in bones and decrease their mother's bone density (NIH, "Pregnancy," 2018).

For teens, the shot comes with this heightened risk, as bone is still depositing at this life stage. With long-term use of this method, teens tend to be at higher risk of losing bone density since their bones are still developing

(Harel et al., 2009). With this in mind, the Depo-Provera company warns its shot should not be used for more than two years. However, controversy arises as major health organizations ACOG and WHO actually refute this warning, arguing the benefits of contraception outweigh its risk of rare bone fracture (KFF, 2020).

<u>Weight Changes</u>
Another consideration for teens is weight gain. Women ages twelve to nineteen were shown to gain an average of five more pounds compared to women taking the pill over the first year. Women who had a high BMI before starting the shot gained about fifteen pounds over the course of a year (Mangan et al., 2002).

Commonly, weight gain is associated with the shot in particular of about two kilograms (or 4.4 pounds), especially among already overweight teens (Mangan et al., 2002). Longer use of the shot may contribute to increased weight gain over time. In a systematic review, the shot was shown to affect body composition. It increased body fat and decreased lean body mass compared to those using non-hormonal contraceptive methods (Lopez et al., 2016).

CONSIDERATIONS
Another systematic review shows women suffering from endometriosis may be offered this contraceptive choice since the research around it, although limited, is promising. Endometriosis, along with its extremely painful nature, is found in 30–50 percent of infertility cases. Although many people associate hormonal contraceptives

with infertility, the shot is especially associated when it is used to treat endometriosis. However, endometriosis on its own is typically associated with infertility. The shot is proven not to affect fertility in the long term. Hormonal contraception can be a powerful tool to help reduce pain, lower menstruation bleeding, and *prolong* fertility. Since progestin limits ovulation, it helps preserve eggs and can potentially help someone plan to have children later in life (Weisberg and Fraser, 2015).

However, the shot can affect short-term fertility. After discontinuing the shot, it takes time for the body to readjust hormone levels—in some cases, up to eighteen months. Other forms of birth control should be considered if the user plans to have children in the near future (Weisberg and Fraser, 2015).

COMMON MISCONCEPTIONS

Misconception: Amenorrhea (no period bleeding) is unnatural and unsafe.

Some people associate lighter, infrequent, or absent periods with abnormality and negative health concerns. However, the medical community instead considers them "healthy and natural" for those using hormonal contraception. Progestins act on the uterus lining, sometimes thinning it to the point where minimal or no bleeding occurs (DeMaria et al., 2019).

The shot offers a significant opportunity for amenorrhea (50 percent of users have no periods), which is, again, safe (Weisberg and Fraser, 2015). To add peace of mind, menstrual changes revert to a person's original baseline within several months after a hormonal contraceptive is discontinued. This has been repeatedly tested and proved in research (Rademacher et al., 2018).

Surely, if one suspects menstruation changes may be a sign of a negative health concern, it is important to rule out other issues. While typical when using hormonal contraception, period changes can signal other reproductive health problems that may be worth investigating with a medical provider. Although it can be tedious for some, tracking periods regularly and taking note of changes can provide valuable insights (NICHD, 2017).

Misconception: The shot causes increased risk of cancer.

Compared to the shot's first market appearance, the shot's ease of use and availability has progressed dramatically. In 1967, the shot was finally released on the market but was denied FDA approval due to scientific allegations that it appeared to cause cancer in animals (Cimons, 1992). However, the shot may have gotten a bad reputation as initial birth control *pill* studies were done with an injectable form on animals first (PBS, 2022). These high-dose formulations injected into these animals caused many health risks, like tumors and infertility (Kaunitz, MD, 2008). Regardless, it seems birth control shot companies had difficulty recovering from the public's fears.

In addition, cervical cancers were becoming more prevalent in the 1960s and 1970s as routine screenings of STIs like HPV became more regular. Today, the CDC has determined 70–90 percent of cervical, anal, vaginal, vulvar, and oropharyngeal cancers are caused by HPV. The quick spread of HPV during the 1960s and 1970s was more likely to blame for increased cervical cancer rates (and other health concerns) than contraception. To this day, we continue to associate cancer-related fears with contraception (Hubacher, 2002).

The shot finally came to market with FDA approval in 1992 after decades of legal battles over these allegedly carcinogenic concerns (Klitsch, 1993). Years of scientific studies, some even conducted by the World Health Organization (WHO), accumulated to prove to the FDA this drug did not increase the risk of cancer. Currently, the shot provides safe and effective contraception to millions of people worldwide. Fortunately, the shot's availability on the market provides an additional option for some people (Westhoff, 2003).

PUTTING IT ALL TOGETHER

With potential side effects in mind, this method provides several great benefits like helping treat endometriosis-associated pain, preventing unintended pregnancy, low invasiveness, and once every three months' administration rather than daily, which may outweigh the risks that come with the aforementioned (typically rare) side effects. The SubQ Depo-Provera option may offer a more desirable approach for patients if they are comfortable administering their own shots.

Insurances tend to cover this method, but if not, it tends to cost about the same as the pill (although a larger sum would be collected every three months rather than spread out monthly). If the patient could not consistently make their appointment every three months, then it may be more beneficial to consider a different option.

Overall, millions of women attain effective contraception from the shot, many decades of research prove its safety, and its notable side effects are reversible.

THE IMPLANT

April 2020: The world was newly shut down, and I was trying to get back in the dating game safely, I hoped. I made last-minute adjustments to my Tinder profile before I started swiping.

I had been sexually active for several years now, each year with its own harrowing episode of questioning whether I was pregnant or not. I stopped before I activated my profile and reflected, *I think it's time in my professional and adult life that I take control of this and stop leaving it up to chance.*

A quick google search brought me to the main contraceptive options. My attention was quickly grabbed by the long-acting reversible contraceptives (LARCs) category. LARCs are among the most effective methods available, yet the hormonal nature provides the widest array of side effects. According to the CDC, "The implant is a single, thin rod that is inserted under the skin of a female's upper arm. The rod contains a progestin that is released in the body over three years. Failure rate: 0.05–0.1 percent." *Extremely effective, excellent!*

I made a consultation appointment right away to get the device.

My doctor sensed I was rushing into the process and asked if I had talked to anyone about the method. I told her I had, though not in-depth. After we set an appointment for the procedure, I called a friend, Edith, who told me she had one in the past.

When Edith initially contemplated her choice of contraceptives, she chose the implant since a couple of her friends had great experiences. One had no more periods after she got the device, and the other friend only had a bit of spotting at first, then very light and regular periods after a few months. She took the gamble and hoped she would turn out like the first friend—no periods, no problems! Sadly, her period experience became horribly sporadic.

Every time she took a trip with friends, she would have to sit out from the hot tub or ocean. Her friends even asked, "Why are you on your period all the time?" She knew they were joking and it was not her fault, but it did frustrate her. Eventually, her doctor suggested putting her on the pill to regulate it, but she decided to have it removed. Overall, her experience was not that bad, and she still recommended that I try it. I hoped I would be one of the lucky ones as well.

I showed up excited and ready for my implant insertion appointment. My doctor started by ordering a pregnancy test and explained the procedure to me. She would inject an anesthetic along my arm, create a small incision, slip in the implant device, and close off the wound. I am a weenie when it comes to needles (shocking because I am a dentist and give injections daily yet cannot stand the sight of them when they are given to me), but I was mentally prepared for this experience. So she began.

My pain tolerance is fairly high, so I could withstand the burn of the injected anesthetic, and my doctor described the steps again as she did them. After the procedure, my doctor had me feel my arm so I could appreciate this new part of me. The rod was made of silicone and was roughly 1.5 inches long, and I could feel its flexible body in mine.

My doctor started giving me instructions to follow, but my world started spinning. I felt faint and interrupted, "Can I sit back down real quick?"

My doctor responded, "Are you feeling vasovagal?"

I sat and focused my eyes on a wall, unable to respond for fear of losing consciousness. My doctor went to get me juice and turned the lights down so I could then relax and normalize my blood pressure.

As I lay there, I felt a humorous memory resurface. I remembered my fond (somewhat traumatic) experience in dental school taking an elective class on inserting IVs.

***

Under direct supervision of a surgical nurse who had been inserting IVs for forty years, my partner and I were instructed to take turns placing an IV in each other's arms.

As the first patient, I watched intently to reinforce the process we had just learned. We were to guide the needle into the vein and leave the plastic catheter in its place. If we did not draw blood the first time, the operator simply had to redirect and re-angle the needle. Our instructor termed this "fishing." My partner had difficulty finding the blood supply in my vein, so in order to find it, our instructor proclaimed, "Ok! Fish for it!" At that point, my world started spinning, I latched on to a thread of consciousness, and our instructor aggressively waved smelling salts in front of my face to keep me awake.

Good times.

***

After I recovered, my doctor warned that if I ever couldn't detect the implant in my arm to let her know. I drove myself home from the hospital. The healing aspect of my implant recovery was minimally inconvenient. I was not in much pain, and my arm only felt mildly sore. My bruise was the size of a smartphone and changed colors every few days until it became hardly noticeable, one month total.

Edith called me after my procedure to follow up on my experience, and I recounted the events for her.

Surprisingly, Edith shared, "Hopefully, everything is uneventful over the next three years for you. I forgot to tell you, but when I finally got mine out, the implant moved around and my doctor had a hard time finding it. They had to take an X-ray to visualize where it was."

After her initial three months of acclimating to her new implant, Edith noticed her implant was not as defined as it was when first placed. She did not stop to consult her doctor on it and simply thought a bit of movement was in the range of normal since it did not hurt. She was more concerned with her irregular menstruation.

Another three months passed, and Edith realized she could barely detect her implant. If she pushed really hard on her arm in the general spot she remembered it placed, she could maybe tell where part of it was. Pushing near that spot on her arm did not help her identify its position. Filled with worry and panic, Edith quickly reached out to her doctor and scheduled an appointment within the week. Her doctor took an X-ray to help locate the general position of the implant and, to Edith's relief, found it was very close to its initial placement site. Her doctor retrieved the device after about thirty minutes, and she healed up within a month.

"Wait, you didn't wanna share this news with me *before* my procedure?" I tried to say jokingly, although she could sense the concern in my voice.

"It was such a rare occurrence; I didn't want it to influence you too much. Honestly, it was my fault to begin with. I should've told my doctor sooner. The surgery to remove it still wasn't bad, and I was worried, but it didn't feel like it took long. It's not like they had to whisk me away to an operating room or anything."

She was right. Difficulty removing the device is a risk, but a rare risk. Honestly, if I had heard this story before my insertion, my initial instinct would have swayed me to avoid this method. I worry about that kind of thinking, considering my level of irrationality behind it. Clouded by fear, making a drastic decision about health seems acceptable in the moment.

MY SIDE EFFECTS

For the first two months, my period was regular in terms of cycle length and was lighter than before. In months three to six, I had no period at all. I remember celebrating myself as being one of the lucky few percentages who no longer to deal with the burden of buying expensive feminine products.

Of course, that came to a sudden halt as months seven through nine changed my cycle from twenty-eight days to a range between eighteen and twenty-five days and *increased* the amount of bleeding I normally experienced. Notably, I was used to having the most predictable menstrual clockwork imaginable.

Months ten through twelve caused me to switch from the implant. My periods went from surprising irregularity to spontaneous fickleness, with no link to my usual pre-period symptoms, at a cycle ranging between seven and thirteen days. I am fortunate I did not struggle with anemia but did have some slight fatigue. After soiling so many clothes at work and bed sheets at home, I realized these hormonal imbalances did not fit my usual routine. After fifteen months of unlucky period changes, I decided to make a switch.

HOW IT WORKS

The implant contraceptive is a small thin rod that contains a progestin (etonogestrel), which thins the uterus lining, prevents egg release, and creates a cervical mucus plug. The only implant currently available on the market is Nexplanon.

To get this method placed, an appointment with a medical provider must be made. They need to numb the inner arm (the patient can choose which arm), make a small incision, slip the implant into the arm, and patch the incision up. This method is now approved to last for three years.

The implant releases a small dose of progestin into the bloodstream over time and continually provides contraceptive effects (Organon, 2021). After three years, it may no longer provide contraception effects and must be removed by a medical provider. However, guidelines are continually evaluated with LARCs, and the window of effectiveness may extend as we collect more data and research.

EFFECTIVENESS

This method is considered the most effective contraceptive method on the market. Its perfect use and typical use effectiveness are over 99 percent. Most of the work for this method is getting it placed, but after that, it does not have to be turned on or off. It does not rely on the user to keep its effectiveness reliable (CDC, 2022).

However, this method does not prevent STIs. Users wishing to delay or prevent pregnancy must additionally use a condom barrier method during sex when a person's partner is inconsistent and/or a current partner's STI status is unknown.

SIDE EFFECTS

Implant Migration

As Edith experienced, implant migration is a possible but very rare occurrence. This mainly causes slight difficulty when locating the implant for removal. People with implants should regularly check their implant placement by feeling their arm for its presence. They should check the implant site often to ensure it remains close to the skin's surface.

If it becomes less detectable, a medical provider should be contacted. Although extremely rare, if the implant ever becomes undetectable, it can necessitate further tests and surgery to locate and remove it so it does not continue to move (Organon, 2021).

Irregular Period Bleeding

Period irregularity is a common side effect, as this method does not contain any synthetic estrogen to temper this.

According to a systematic review, 77 percent of people do not have problems with their period after three months. Period changes can be noted for six to twelve months following insertion. Light bleeding or heavy bleeding can occur. Although amenorrhea (no period) can occur, it may only be for a limited window of time (Mansour et al., 2008). If period changes seem unacceptable, a different choice should be considered.

CONSIDERATIONS

After the insertion procedure, some soreness in the arm is expected for about one to two weeks. A medical provider may recommend taking some over-the-counter pain medications before the procedure (and possibly after) to help with discomfort. While the initial incision heals, it is rare but possible for the implant to get pushed out. If this were to happen, the implant would no longer work as an effective contraceptive. During the initial healing phase, the user should make sure to keep the area protected until the skin heals over it.

Bruising in that area is very noticeable after the insertion and may take about four to six weeks to resolve. Although it tends to blend in and the inner aspect of the arm is not typically seen in photos, some scarring may remain, which may not be preferable for some.

It is important for the user to keep track of the date their implant was inserted. Sometimes people transfer medical services due to relocation or insurance changes. It is important to remember when the implant is due for replacement.

Initially, I liked the area the in which the implant was placed. This newly vulnerable inner part of my arm felt safe and protected during the healing phase. Looking back, I wished I had considered the fact that I did a fair amount of yoga throughout the week, specifically poses like crow pose where my knees rest the weight of my body on that area. If too much force is applied to the implant, it may bend or break. Although rare, if this happens, a healthcare provider should be contacted (Organon, 2021).

COMMON MISCONCEPTIONS
Misconception: Irregular period bleeding should be routinely treated.

Irregular period bleeding is common with this method and causes no need for concern. Since a provider is needed to place the device, they will usually map out their patient's reproductive health status in advance. Likely, bleeding disturbances following implant placement do not indicate a negative health issue.

For some people, an irregular period is annoying yet manageable. Unlucky users who fall into this camp usually can deal with the irregularities and prepare by always having period products around.

For some people, frequently irregular bleeding is unacceptable. A systematic review shows people can benefit from these strategies: getting a prescription for a medication containing estrogen or taking over-the-counter pain medications (only if instructed by a medical provider). While these methods work for some, research does not support treating irregular bleeding regularly, as they have not been proven to work in larger studies (Abdel-Aleem et al., 2013).

Misconception: Since the implant is the most novel contraceptive method invented, it likely has many flaws.

While Nexplanon is the only implant on the market currently, several iterations of implants have been released on the market and studied. The first implant was FDA-approved in 1990. It was called Norplant. The first generation had six progestin-containing rods, and the second had two rods. It was removed from the market in 2002 due to its complications and questionable effectiveness (KFF, 2019).

A different company gained FDA approval and released a second implant in 2006 called Implanon, which also contained the etonogestrel progestin. They instead designed this implant to be a single rod. It was much more effective and easier to place and remove. In 2010, this same company removed this generation from the market, replacing it with its second-generation implant, Nexplanon, which uses the same progestin. The main differences are its visibility on X-ray and the improved application tool. Much of the research we have from the first generation applies to the current implant since it uses the same progestin (KFF, 2019).

PUTTING IT ALL TOGETHER

Aside from my (relatively minor) frustrations, I still felt an overwhelming sense of peace with this contraceptive option. I did not want to be pregnant yet, and guess what, I did not get pregnant! I wished I had done more research before choosing this contraceptive since it would impact my daily life. At the very least, I should have inquired more about other people's experiences before making my decision.

Most people using this method report no sustained problems and end up highly satisfied. Although some side effects can be worrisome initially, most side effects are similar to other progestin-only methods. Some people are more comfortable with the idea of a device inserted in their arm rather than in their vagina or uterus. This method can provide a middle ground for invasiveness.

I know several people who are very satisfied and happy with this method, and they tell me they are excited to get their current ones replaced with the implant again after their three-year expiration date hits. They enjoy not having to remember anything for their contraception to work highly effectively, no matter how busy or tame their schedules may be.

HORMONAL IUDS

Serena felt like her life was in constant flux. She felt overwhelmed juggling her nursing night classes, her full-time barista job, and her dating life. Each time she was in a new romantic relationship, she realized she kept putting off going on birth control. She would lie next to her partner and hope she was not pregnant. *I feel so dumb. I'm so close to finishing school, and I don't want to postpone my career any longer,* she thought. She felt her family, her school counselors, and society in general did not expect her to succeed.

She was always told she had to work ten times harder than others, and her family couldn't provide any safety net or savings. Whenever she felt this sense of hopelessness, she would think back to an important memory in her life, when a teacher from her freshman year of high school, Ms. Denise, inspired her to take matters into her own hands.

***

Ms. Denise offered her classroom as a place of refuge to Serena and other students. She provided snacks and even a "comfort corner" for weary students to de-stress. Serena often felt fatigued by the demands of school, and some days felt she hardly lived up to mediocre expectations. After observing the sullen way Serena often held herself in class, Ms. Denise took a chance on Serena and said, "What kind of life would you want for yourself if you could?"

"Why does it matter?" Serena paused. "A good job, I guess."

"Serena, I think you can get more out of life if you wanted to. I'm not saying you have to know what that is right now, but I believe you can."

"Can what?"

"People in your life will always try to tell you what you should do, but I want you to remember you can decide what you can do."

Serena thought about this but ultimately shrugged it off and asked, "Well, can I leave now?"

Ms. Denise nodded, unaware of the lasting impact she had on Serena.

***

Thinking back on this memory, Serena remembered she could do something about her current situation. She could go on birth control and delay pregnancy until she was ready. This was her life. She decided to ask some of her close nursing school friends what contraceptives they used. Strangely enough, they all shared they had hormonal IUDs. Many of them also worked on the side and had extremely unpredictable schedules. Most other forms of contraceptives did not offer the opportunity to "set and forget" like the hormonal IUD did. A reliable method independent of constant reminders felt ideal.

Serena felt comfortable considering this option, as her friends shared mostly positive experiences. She made an appointment to get a consultation on the IUD first. She preferred to know as many facts as possible before starting something new.

During her next free afternoon, she made a video appointment with the OBGYN clinic. As she logged on to the clinic's video conference, she sat looking back at herself in the virtual waiting room, grateful she did not have to take a full day off just to learn more about hormonal IUDs.

The video screen switched on, revealing Dr. Walsh on the other line. She waved on the screen in greeting. "Hey, Serena! So good to meet you virtually! I see that on your forms, you mentioned you're a nursing student *and* barista at Jill's Coffee full time. How do you do it?"

"Honestly, I wouldn't be here if it wasn't for the free coffee," Serena joked.

Dr. Walsh laughed and said, "What can I help you with today?"

Serena responded, "It's like you said, I feel like I'm always busy, and I know nursing school is about to turn up several notches of difficulty soon. I've wanted to be a nurse ever since I was in high school. Now I am so close to finally reaching that dream, but I'm not ready for pregnancy yet. I want to learn more about the hormonal IUD."

"A lot of healthcare workers use IUDs. It's definitely beneficial for people with schedules that are all over the place."

"How is it placed? And does it hurt?

"Placement is simple and can be done during a routine visit; it doesn't involve surgery. It will be uncomfortable for the initial placement and will feel like you're having pretty severe cramps the next day. I'll have you take some pain medications before the visit so it's not as bad."

"That all sounds good to me. Is there anything else you think would be good for me to know?" asked Serena.

Dr. Walsh said, "Well, there are two major types of IUDs—hormonal and non-hormonal, or the copper. Do you plan to have children in the near future?"

"If everything goes according to plan, hopefully I could have kids after nursing school."

"Would you be open to the hormonal IUD? I personally like that option since your periods can lighten and sometimes stop while it's in, and it is completely safe to do so."

Serena gasped, "Oh, really? That would be one less thing to worry about so long as it's safe."

"I can send you additional information before the procedure to make sure we covered everything. But as far as next steps, you can call our reception and schedule the procedure when you're ready."

"Thanks, Dr. Walsh. Appreciate you."

They both waved into the camera and shut off their videos.

Serena scheduled her insertion appointment with excitement. She felt proud she could take matters into her own hands. Ms. Denise would be proud too. She was capable.

***

Serena's story was inspired by a combination of a few of my friend's contraceptive journeys. Many busy people have unpredictable schedules. Relying on a method that requires a strict routine for full effectiveness seemed too inconceivable to them. Many LARCs (long-acting reversible contraceptives) provide this peace of mind, and the hormonal IUD is popular for several reasons we will explore.

HOW IT WORKS
IUD Components and Procedures

Two types of intrauterine devices (IUDs) exist on the market. The first type is hormonal IUDs, which contain progestin hormones, and the second type is the copper IUD, which is non-hormonal (we will discuss this type in detail next chapter).

To understand how IUDs work, we can break down their components. First, IUDs are T-shaped. The horizontal arms of the T are the plastic frame responsible for holding the device in place near the base (or the deeper end) of the uterus. The vertical body of the T holds progestin hormones (or copper ions) and points toward the cervix. Threads are attached to the end of the vertical T, opposite the horizontal arms, and are designed to hang below the cervix for removal.

The doctor can teach the patient how to periodically check for these strings in order to check its position. Some partners can feel these ends during sex, but the ends do not cause discomfort or issues. This could be a plus since the partner could help check the IUD is in its proper place.

IUDs come in a thin, sterile insertion tube. During insertion, the provider will place the tube into the uterus, allow the arms to open, position the IUD, remove the tube, and cut the excess threads, leaving about half an inch remaining from the opening of the cervix (Bayer, 2008).

When a patient decides on an IUD for contraception, they schedule two appointments with their provider—one to screen and one to insert the device. At the initial screening visit, the provider can establish a health baseline with the patient, review consent forms, answer questions about the procedure, and perform STI and pregnancy tests. Prior to the second procedure visit, taking pain killers may also be suggested to help with the recovery.

Once at the clinic, the provider will likely start with a pregnancy test again and review health information. The procedure then begins when the patient undresses and sits on the table, resting their feet up and apart on the footrests. The clinician may examine the area and assess the length of the cervix using a speculum (a long, metal tool that holds the reproductive tube open to gain visualization). The clinician may also use local anesthetics to make the procedure more comfortable.

The device can be removed at the end of its expiration date, or it can be removed earlier if the patient's life circumstances change (such as wanting to have a pregnancy) or even if they are simply dissatisfied with the method itself.

Once the patient decides they would like the device removed, they can schedule an appointment with their healthcare provider. The provider simply uses an instrument to retrieve the IUD's strings and pulls the device out. The horizontal arms collapse, and the process is generally more comfortable and easier to recover from than the insertion.

Specific Hormonal IUDs
Four types of hormonal IUDs are currently available in the US:

- Mirena
- LILETTA
- Skyla
- Kyleena

Hormonal IUDs have similar effects and designs. As a review, progestin hormones are responsible for contraceptive effects (thinning uterus walls, preventing egg release, thickening cervical mucus). The progestin used in these devices is levonorgestrel (LNG). Hormonal IUDs differ slightly in their amount of LNG and in size (although all are about the size of a half-dollar coin).

Mirena and LILETTA are slightly larger devices and contain more progestin.

<u>Mirena</u> is effective as a birth control method for seven years; it is effective for other contraceptive effects (such as helping decrease heavy periods) for five years (Bayer: Mirena, 2022).

<u>LILETTA</u> is effective for six years. It was created by a nonprofit called Medicines360 and a socially responsible company called Afaxys. They offer discounts for people with lower incomes at clinics enrolled in the government's 340B Drug Pricing Program (more information on finding these clinics in the Resources section).

Skyla and Kyleena have slightly smaller dimensions, which may be more comfortable in smaller uteruses.

<u>Skyla</u> is effective for three years (Bayer: Skyla, 2021).

Kyleena is effective for five years, although it interestingly has the smallest design and least progestin (Bayer: Kyleena, 2021).

EFFECTIVENESS

Although they differ slightly in their marketing approach, hormone amount, and hormone release strategy, they all have equal effectiveness during the entirety of their approved life span. With perfect use, hormonal IUDs are over 99 percent effective, and with typical use are also over 99 percent effective (Bedsider, 2019). Pregnancy prevention here is as effective as sterilization. This might be a great option for those who want to reliably prevent unintended pregnancy but don't want to completely severe the option of pregnancy in the future.

Although the Mirena IUD is technically the only FDA-approved IUD listed to reduce menstrual bleeding, all hormonal IUDs may be effective in helping reduce cramping and/or heavy periods associated with female reproductive issues like endometriosis (Weisberg and Fraser, 2015). As I repeatedly recommend, the best practice in choosing a particular IUD involves consulting a medical doctor.

Lastly, this method is highly effective at preventing pregnancy but offers no protection from STIs. For those using hormonal IUDs, a female or male condom must be used during sex to prevent STIs (Bedsider, 2019).

Patients considering hormonal IUDs have several risks to consider, such as irregular periods (such as spotting and breakthrough bleeding) and ovarian cysts. With the hormonal IUD, patients often experience lighter periods (OASH, 2019).

Although the exact mechanism is not well understood, levonorgestrel is highly effective at reducing and sometimes eliminating period bleeding (amenorrhea), perhaps due to effectively thinning the uterine walls. Compared to other hormonal methods, patients using hormonal IUDs have a higher chance of complete amenorrhea after one year:

- Mirena – 20 percent,
- LILETTA – 20 percent,
- Kyleena – 12 percent,
- Skyla – 6 percent (University Health Services, 2019).

The risk of ovarian cysts in the first three to six months after placement spontaneously resolves within a few months without any intervention (Nahum et al., 2015). However, the current research on this could be potentially skewed since they typically study a small sample of people who are already experiencing reproductive health issues. In other words, perhaps more people who do not have the opportunity to come in for more frequent medical visits would show they have benign ovarian cysts from time to time without any noticeable symptoms (Ross and Kebria, 2013). The risk of developing ovarian cysts to the point where it bothers patients is very low, and routine ultrasounds are not necessary (Kailasam and Cahill, 2008).

CONSIDERATIONS

The IUD insertion process may seem intimidating at first, but with planning and realistic expectations, this can be managed well. For example, a person can plan a rest day after their insertion to focus on healing and relaxing during the most intense pain. They can also ask their doctor about pain management techniques, like heating pads and pain medications.

Once inserted, the hormonal IUD takes time to reach full effectiveness as the female reproductive system needs time for the IUD hormones to signal changes. The patient's doctor can give a more complete picture of how long it will take to reach full effectiveness since it depends on the type of contraceptive used prior and the number of days since the last menstrual cycle (Scully and Nwadike, MD, MPH, 2021).

Each of the hormonal IUDs has an approved length of effective use, meaning effectiveness cannot be guaranteed after the expiration date. Sometimes people change clinics, cities, or states after their IUD is inserted, and it may be difficult for a new provider to identify when the removal date should be without prior records. It may be up to the patient to remember when they had the insertion and request removal when the time comes.

IUDs are not for everyone, especially if they have various preexisting conditions such as:

- Pregnancy, or suspected pregnancy
- Sexually transmitted infection at the time of insertion
- A congenital uterine abnormality that distorts the shape of the uterine cavity
- Acute pelvic inflammatory disease
- History of pelvic inflammatory disease, unless a subsequent successful intrauterine pregnancy has occurred
- History of septic abortion or history of postpartum endometritis within the last three months
- Confirmed or suspicion of uterine or cervical cancer
- Abnormal uterine bleeding of unknown origin
- Any condition that increases the risk of pelvic infection
- History of previously inserted IUD that has not been removed
- Hypersensitivity to any component of the device

Unique contraindications for hormonal IUDs include:

- Confirmed or suspicion of breast malignancy or other progestin-sensitive cancer
- Liver tumors, benign or malignant
- Acute liver disease (Lanzola and Ketvertis, 2021).

The importance of keeping medical providers up to date on current medical status cannot be stressed enough.

COMMON MISCONCEPTIONS

For many people, the idea of a device inserted into their uterus can seem dangerous, foreign, and invasive. The media has added to our clouded judgment due to infamous yet isolated historical events. In addressing our preconceived conceptions, it is important to understand where IUD stigmas originate and rewrite their history.

Misconception: IUDs were only just developed in the twenty-first century.

Methods to prevent pregnancy were devised in ancient times to prevent ancient sperm from meeting ancient eggs. Tales of natural spermicide concoctions and physical barriers made of animal skins have been recorded (PBS, 2022). Although legends of tools blocking the uterus to prevent pregnancy exist, highly predictable methods were not created in sophisticated forms (that we know of) until the early twentieth century.

In 1906, Dr. Richard Richter was credited with the first documented intrauterine device (IUD) using silkworm gut rings to block sperm from the entrance of the uterus (Margulies, 1975). After decades of failed attempts and design iterations, people suffered ailments from early IUD products such as gingival argyrosis (bluish-black gums from absorbing silver), painful cramps and bleeding, device ejection, damage to the uterus and cervix through device perforation, and, less frequently, cancer and infertility thought to be due to aggressive insertion methods. Still, some researchers had successful clinical results but no way to broadcast their innovations to the scientific community due to the limitations of the Comstock laws. These laws made it illegal to spread "obscene" or "indecent" information in the mail, banning the spread of contraceptive information even if a doctor wrote it (Burnette, 2009).

Over time, women became even more desperate to control their reproductive health. The cries of women were heard globally. The Population Council arose in the 1950s as an international, evidence-based nonprofit dedicated to developing biomedical products to ethically serve developing countries. They published important research highlighting prevalent issues: unintended overpopulation was depleting already-scarce resources and family planning solutions were simply not accessible, though desperately needed. In 1962, the Population Council held the first international IUD conference, inviting fifty researchers to collaborate on their IUD designs and methods.

In 1969, Dr. Howard Tatum created a comfortable plastic T-shaped device to address the copious discomfort concerns of early IUDs that were generally too large or made of over-reactive materials. Concurrently, Dr. Jaime Zipper in Chile discovered the contraceptive effects of copper in the uterus. In 1970, Dr. Antonio Scommegna created a T-shaped progesterone IUD, which was approved and sold in the market for over thirty years. As effectiveness and ease of use gained traction, companies heavily marketed IUDs and many women flocked to this method (RHAP, 2013).

Misconception: IUDs cause deadly infections.

Ten percent of women using contraception in the 1970s used IUDs, yet, by the turn of the century, only two percent of contraception users had IUDs. Why the dramatic decline? The popularity of IUDs was at an all-time high when the A.H. Robins Company's Dalkon Shield IUD came to the market in 1971 (Hubacher, 2002). The negative associations and fears of the IUD stem from this particular device.

To set the stage, we must remember the social climate of the 1970s. This was the time of "free love," where people using IUDs were engaging in riskier sexual activities compared to previous decades, resulting in higher STI susceptibility and incidence.

Several issues with research were prevalent back then too. Pelvic inflammatory disease (PID) was likely over-diagnosed in IUD users. PID is a serious infection of the female reproductive system, which creates a range of female health complications like infertility. Those with IUDs were more likely to seek medical attention when a fertility problem appeared, whereas others with infertility problems may have just blamed themselves and did not seek medical attention. People lacked the education to seek help for suspected fertility issues, and the data in early research studies were skewed, incorrectly associating IUDs with PID (Hubacher, 2002).

This brings us to the release of the Dalkon Shield. This IUD was aggressively marketed as this revolutionarily designed, highly effective, ingeniously novel contraceptive. Women eagerly pushed to attain their Dalkon

Shields, even switching from their effective prior method. As more women tried it, cases of infection rose. PID, infertility, sepsis, and even seven deaths were reported. The A.H. Robins Company denied allegations, hid facts, and continued selling and pushing their product en masse (Hubacher, 2002).

The source of these problems was a design flaw in the device. The retrieval strings were made up of a threaded material that allowed bacteria from the vaginal canal to travel up the device and cause infection (similar to toxic shock syndrome when tampons are left in for too long). Finally, when the scandal was revealed, the US Senate intervened, declaring the Dalkon Shield harmful. Mass media covered this scandal, showing accounts of women crying out about feelings of betrayal. They originally thought this device would bring them a sense of peace, protection, and control, only to find it brought them horror, infection, and death. Many women had their IUDs removed and remained fearful of all IUDs (Hubacher, 2002).

The increased susceptibility to infection from STI spread, the over-reported incidence of PID in IUD users, and the traumatizing experience of women who used the Dalkon Shield resulted in the lingering IUD associations of infection and infertility we have today. These negative outcomes are simply not caused by the IUDs now on the market.

Now, IUD use in America is steadily gaining popularity again as safety is enforced and research is improved.

Roughly 8 percent of contraception users in the US use IUDs. However, compared to other developed countries (e.g., Korea 49 percent, Europe 17–27 percent), the US has lower rates. Likely, this is due to these lingering Dalkon Shield stigmas. With less interest in IUDs, the US has fallen behind in IUD research when we see other countries continually push to design new IUD products to address women's needs (Beaton, 2017).

As we continue to educate on IUD safety, the use of this method is expected to continue to rise. Now, dozens of current high-quality research studies help prove IUD safety and effectiveness. Gynecologists and other healthcare professionals use it themselves at a much higher rate than the general public, with high satisfaction (Sonfield, 2007).

PUTTING IT ALL TOGETHER

All in all, hormonal IUDs are a highly effective method. Since each of the available hormonal IUDs has a different expiration date, consider the timeline for having the next child. Some other considerations here include comfort level with reducing periods, amount of hormone contained in the device, and uterus size (possibly related to history of past childbirth).

Although different clinics may not have all IUD brands in stock, the specific device chosen will be determined by conversations with a partnering doctor. With the growing rate of popularity of this method, more hormonal IUD methods may enter into the selection and provide additional reliable methods to choose from.

THE COPPER IUD

Here we go again, I thought, *and now my doctor knows I will have an intense recovery reaction after* (so embarrassing!), *but it will all be worth it so I don't have to deal with tampering with my hormones after a few months.*

I scheduled a big appointment for myself on one of my few and precious days off: removal of my Nexplanon implant and insertion of the copper IUD, Paragard. I was excited to see my pleasant and charming OBGYN in person again. She had been emailing me and video conferencing with me, talking through the various side effects I was experiencing. We both had hoped my case would be a successful one, where I would go about my normal life with little or no period, lessened acne, and peace of mind avoiding unintended pregnancy. But here we were, agreeing it was time to switch methods since I could not tolerate my hormonal side effects.

My periods were more frequent and heavier, my acne was pretty much non-existent (sad to give this up), and my skin dried out, contributing to eczema flares.

I felt comforted switching to the copper IUD since it was also a highly effective method similar to the implant (99.6 percent vs. 99.9 percent) (CDC, 2022). When I first selected the implant, I remembered seeing this marginal difference in effectiveness online and allowed it to guide my decision without much critical thought. It always interested me that in medicine, people would be willing to spend over 500 percent more on a procedure that would nudge their success rate an additional 0.3 percent. This is in part why medical technology companies are so lucrative.

If I was going to buy a car that had an extra 0.3 percent safety rating because of a special seat belt mechanism and the difference would be an extra ten thousand dollars on top of the price of the car, forget it, I would take my chances! Also, I realized the 0.3 percent difference may also be due to less data on the implant since it was released on the market in 2006, while the copper IUD was released in 1988 (KFF, 2019).

My doctor walked into the room and caught up with me a bit; she likes getting right into the procedure, but I love talking to her since her field is everything I like to research. She told me, "I'm surprised how many people believe periods are necessary for 'cleansing' the body for religious or personal beliefs."

I asked, "What's a common misconception you think most patients have?"

She replied, "People assume we have to have periods for proper health. However, we don't need periods, and they don't determine our fertility. My med school friends and I love our hormonal IUDs since we don't like having periods."

We started with the implant removal after our brief discussion, and she informed me the implant had drifted a bit, but not much, so she was going to try to use the same incision mark to retrieve it. Of course, as she told me what was happening, I blocked out the thought of it to shut out my queasiness, but I ended up focusing on what she was saying anyway since I had nothing else to focus on. She numbed the area with lidocaine—"Pinch and burn!"—and the rest I couldn't feel. I knew something was going on, but it just felt like my arm was moving slightly, and I sensed pressure.

My mind tried to wander, and I asked her something else about the birth control pill and—

"It's out! Wanna see?"

I didn't look at it the first time, so I said, "Sure!"

There it was, a thin, short, white stick that caused me over a year of inconvenience. She patched me up and said, "The implant is easy to put in but takes a bit to remove it, and the IUD is the opposite!"

Oh, great... I didn't realize I had stacked two difficult procedures on the same day, I thought. Next, we moved our attention to my vagina. I put my feet up on the footrests and had a drape over my lower half, forming a little privates' tent. The nurse gave me a heating pad and placed it on my abdomen.

"What's this for?" I asked.

"For the cramps."

'Ok, I can handle cramps. I've dealt with them my whole life.'

My doctor then asked, "Did you bring headphones? You can listen to music if I want some distraction."

I told her, "No, thanks." I wanted to remember everything that happened.

Although I could not see the procedure, I felt the insertion of the speculum. It was slightly uncomfortable but not bad at all. I felt the injection, which was more of an uncomfortable pressure. I did not like this, but it was definitely manageable. The worst part (I think) was the initial placement of the IUD.

My doctor said, "You might be feeling faint. It's a very common experience when your cervix is touched."

I feel nauseous, too, I thought. I could not speak through my discomfort. The cramps started right away, but my senses were mixed. I did not know if this was a reaction to the procedure itself or my body adjusting to my new IUD. Regardless, my doctor knew I would need a moment (or several) to recover. She had me stay on the examination table, brought me water, and dimmed the lights.

Nurses checked on me periodically to ensure I was recovering rather than forcing myself to leave before I was ready (they worried I would pass out in the lobby, where it would be difficult to care for me and readmit me). After about twenty minutes of sitting in my uncomfortable cramps, I pushed myself to drive home.

As I drove, the pain of my cramps ramped up. The only thing I could do when I got home was lay on my couch; I felt dizzy from the pain. Curled up with my heating pad on my stomach, I forced myself to sleep to escape its intensity the rest of the day.

I had to take over-the-counter pain medication, as instructed, every six hours for the following three days to manage the pain, and I felt the pain return around the five-hour mark regardless. The pain was hardly noticeable by day three, but I continued my pain medications for two more days in fear of the pain returning.

I felt the side effects from my Nexplanon implant start to resolve after two weeks into the switch. Perhaps it was only a placebo effect, but I felt the brain fog from my previous hormonal contraceptive disappear completely too. I also had some resolution of my painfully severe dry skin. It took about four full months for my period to finally regulate back to normal, and I couldn't escape the common side effect of heavier period bleeding. Each start of my menstrual phase brought on slightly more intense cramps than I remembered having before. My period cycle length decreased, causing me to bleed every three weeks for seven days rather than every four weeks for five days due to increased spotting.

All in all, I was very pleased with my choice. The copper IUD did not give me any curveball side effects, and now I was confident and overjoyed I had control over my reproductive health.

HOW IT WORKS

Since this method is also an IUD, it has a similar T-shape to the hormonal IUDs. The main difference is the vertical part of the T. Instead of holding the chamber of hormones, it has a body of copper.

Unique to the copper IUD, the copper component is responsible for the copper IUD's highly effective contraceptive action. Its presence triggers a local inflammatory response in the body, killing sperm in the process. The copper ions mix into the cervical mucus, making it difficult to enter the uterus and disrupting the sperm's swimming ability. Lastly, the copper changes the uterine lining and creates a toxic environment for sperm, inactivating their functionality (Kaneshiro and Aeby, 2010).

One of the main benefits of this option is its non-hormonal nature. Since the hormonal cycle is not affected and ovulation is not blocked, the user can become pregnant as soon as the device is removed. Another benefit of the copper IUD is its lifespan. It can be in place for ten years with full effectiveness over that time. More research in the near future will likely prove effectiveness for a few additional years, but currently, the FDA approves ten. For those not interested in having (more) children, only having to worry about one medical appointment every ten years can be advantageous (CooperSurgical, 2021).

EFFECTIVENESS

Similar to hormonal IUDs, the copper IUD is over 99 percent effective. Typical use has about 0.8 percent failure, whereas perfect use would be 0.6 percent failure. The slight discrepancy here has to do with a rare clinical insertion error. Surprisingly (or maybe unsurprisingly), many medical doctors were not trained to insert IUDs in their initial training programs, considering the relative novelty of the device (released in 1988). Since each training program differs, providers have various familiarity with the insertion technique (Bedsider, 2019).

Furthermore, patients in certain regions may be less interested in IUD contraceptives, which leaves clinicians less inclined to recommend them. According to research findings from the American College of Obstetricians and Gynecologists, with proper and effective counseling, IUDs become more enticing to patients. Strategies to increase access, like incorporating an all-inclusive-one-visit placement, are now being pushed to the table (ACOG, 2018).

Every year, more clinical training is implemented into programs as demand for long-acting contraception grows, and providers are becoming more comfortable suggesting and placing this contraceptive option (Luchowski, 2014).

The copper IUD is also the most effective emergency contraception, with 99.9 percent effectiveness if inserted within five days after unprotected sex. It is thought to block implantation since the uterus lining is changed, but the mechanism of action is not fully understood. The downside is a clinician has to insert the device, and an appointment may not be as readily available as other emergency contraceptives (more on this in the emergency contraceptive chapter) (Bedsider, 2019).

Lastly, the copper IUD does not effectively provide any STI protection.

SIDE EFFECTS

The most common side effect to consider is heavier menstrual cramps, especially for a few days after insertion, due to the inflammatory nature of the device. Additionally, patients typically experience heavier periods and sometimes spotting between periods as well. This may not be a great option for those who already suffer from painful cramps and heavy flows.

Extremely rare side effects can include embedment, perforation, and expulsion (CooperSurgical, 2021). Embedment means part of the IUD can get stuck to the uterus. Often, this goes unnoticed in the IUD user but would make removing the IUD more difficult, possibly requiring minimal surgical intervention. Perforation means the IUD may cause a puncture in the uterus (a one in one thousand chance). Expulsion means the IUD can start to come out of the uterus (essentially, the uterus pushes the IUD down, revealing part or all of the IUD). This may not be a painful experience, but it can result in cramping, bleeding, or discomfort. Expulsion can be more likely (but still rare) in individuals who have a larger uterus from giving birth (Ray, DNP and Wahl, 2020).

As soon as discomfort is associated with the IUD, a doctor should be notified. They can take an X-ray to check the position of the IUD.

Regardless, the IUD should not move on its own (Tighe, 2015). Negative experiences are more commonly shared publicly than positive experiences. These rare circumstances tend to seem common but are not a true representation. Think of online reviews where customers want to share complaints to possibly influence other buyers or try to get refunds on their products. Those happy with their product are less likely to publicly share their positive experience.

CONSIDERATIONS

A medical doctor is needed to insert the device. Often, this takes two appointments: one for the consultation and one for the insertion. Fortunately, the advances of telehealth have allowed many institutions to reduce the number of in-person visits. However, if weekday time is a rare commodity, clinical appointments can be challenging to attain in a timely manner.

Individuals should not use this method if they have pre-existing conditions (listed in the hormonal IUDs chapter), such as pregnancy or active reproductive system infection. Lastly, any form of copper sensitivity would be grounds to consider a different option.

COMMON MISCONCEPTION
Misconception: The copper IUD is highly linked to infection.

The copper IUD follows the same historical path as the hormonal IUD. The fate of the copper IUD branches from the hormonal IUD with the clever addition of copper.

The effects of copper were accidentally discovered in the mid-1920s when researchers experimented with inserted ring-shaped devices. Ernst Gräfenberg coiled silver wire (contaminated by copper) into his device and found it highly effective. This was a highly popular device in England but did not gain traction in the US due to misconceived fears of infection, pain, and cancer associated with IUD history. In 1962, the effects of copper were formally discovered by two biomedical researchers of the Population Council, whose individual findings resulted in this method. Dr. Jaime Zipper discovered metallic copper effects, and Dr. Howard Tatum incorporated it into his T-shaped device (Margulies, MD, 1975).

In 1976, the first copper IUD gained FDA approval, and it was the first time a new drug application was sponsored by a nonprofit research organization dedicated to serving global family planning concerns, the Population Council (Population Council, 2022).

At one point, this was the most popular and safe birth control method available, but this early copper IUD, and most other IUDs, were taken off the market after the tragic Dalkon Shield scandal. The public lost faith in the IUD contraceptive. In 1988, the Paragard (Copper T 380A) reemerged as a viable option with safe nylon retrieval strings rather than the flawed, bacteria-harboring Dalkon Shield retrieval strings (CooperSurgical, 2021).

Paragard remains the only copper IUD approved in the US.

A very, very small risk of PID is possible within the first few weeks of insertion. This can occur because of the placement procedure, which may (very rarely) cause the transmission of bacteria from the vaginal canal to deeper tissues in the reproductive system (OASH, 2019).

When we think about this risk, we must compare it to the risk of PID during pregnancy, which is much higher. Even mild dental procedures like fillings have a risk of transmitting bacterial infection from the mouth to deeper tissues. While very rare as well, they can happen. The benefits of preventing pregnancy-associated health concerns outweigh the rare risks for this method.

PUTTING IT ALL TOGETHER

Ultimately, the copper IUD is the most effective, non-hormonal, reversible contraception available in the US. Although appointments may be tough to schedule, the procedure itself may seem frightening, and the recovery may be uncomfortable, this method effectively and predictably lasts for ten years. A common strategy people implement when they are done having children is copper IUD insertion, which can sometimes carry them through menopause.

Hormonal methods come with a significant range of reported side effects. The copper IUD may be an underused method with a bad reputation (for no fault of its own). For those weary of the effects of hormones on their bodies, this could be a more advantageous and effective long-term option.

STERILIZATION

Terri was a thirty-one-year-old mother of two. She had a three-year-old daughter who loved dragons and climbing playground rock walls, and she had a one-year-old son who loved sunglasses and crawling on colorful carpets. Motherhood made Terri selfless, strong, and patient. She had a brilliant way of describing the world in childlike terms. Her friends had a profound respect for her maturity, and they would often ask for her parenting and relationship advice. Terri inadvertently found people confiding in her, even if they had only just met. Whether it was the surprising mix of her gentle nature and candor, or her genuine, active listening skills, other mothers found comfort and peace in their discussions with Terri.

Terri and her best friend Theresa would talk daily. Terri never ran out of patience to answer Theresa's questions, from "what should I do about my son Billy getting caught cheating at school?" to "how do I get my husband Pete to stand up for me in front of his mother?" Terri had the wisdom to help her friend navigate through her life, yet she found it difficult to navigate her own issues with her reproductive health.

Terri and her husband David were open to growing their family, but Terri's last two pregnancies were very difficult on her. She had been bedridden for months at a time. After the birth of their second child, Terri's doctor, Dr. Yao, solemnly warned another pregnancy could be even more difficult, to the point where her life could be at risk, and David feared for his wife's life. Deeply concerned, he told her, "Your life is too important to me and the kids to risk. We can explore other ways to grow our family that still keep you safe."

Dr. Yao detected the couple's sense of urgency and started listing options to help them prevent another pregnancy. He explained, "Long-acting reversible contraceptive options are reliable forms of contraception. They are over 99 percent effective, comparable to sterilization. The hormonal methods work for three to six years, while the copper IUD works for about ten years."

Terri asked, "So when I'm forty-one, I'd have to get another method placed?"

"Correct," Dr. Yao said.

He continued, "A more long-term option you two can consider is sterilization, which is highly effective, again, over 99 percent, and irreversible. I'll explain the procedure, and then I have to inform you of the rare risks. The female version includes general anesthesia, an incision through the naval area, and navigating to the fallopian tubes to cut them. Healing can take days to weeks. Also,

for the female method, there is still a rare risk of an ectopic pregnancy."

"What's an ectopic pregnancy?" David asked.

"A pregnancy that starts in a non-uterine place. In this
case, the ectopic pregnancy would start in the fallopian
tubes, but with all pregnancies, there is a chance for ectopic pregnancy. In reality, sterilization technically lowers
the overall risk of ectopic pregnancy."

The couple sat puzzled and fearful, considering
this information.

Dr. Yao pressed on, "Male sterilization, or the vasectomy,
includes local anesthesia, an incision or two on the scrotum, and navigating to the vasa deferentia (the tubes
where sperm travel before they are released) to cut them.
For the male method, full effectiveness is not reached
until four months later since it takes time for all the
sperm to clear out" (ACOG, March 2019).

"It sounds like the male procedure is less invasive," David
surmised.

"That's usually the case, but all surgeries inherently have
a risk of complications and require recovery time," Dr.
Yao replied.

"Terri has been through a lot for our family. I think it's my
turn to share this responsibility," David stated.

***

Women like Terri have troubling issues with their reproductive health. We must remember our reproductive health and overall health are intertwined.

Terri and David's story is a composite story inspired by a few friends' experiences as couples. Dr. Yao adeptly covered the main overarching topics of this method, and we will expand on the information he presented.

HOW IT WORKS

For females, two categories of sterilization procedures exist; one requires an operational surgery and one does not. Surgical sterilization procedures can either be performed through minilaparotomy (surgeon uses their direct vision) or laparoscopy (surgeon uses a scope to visualize). Both require putting the patient under general anesthesia and making a small incision to access and block (or remove) the fallopian tubes (ACOG, August 2019).

Although no longer available on the market, a nonsurgical intervention called Essure was inserted through the vagina and deposited in the fallopian tubes to block eggs and sperm from meeting. However, this method took several months to reach effectiveness and stopped sales in 2018 (Bayer, 2020).

For males, two categories of sterilization procedures also exist; one requires two incisions and one requires a small puncture (a no-scalpel method). The incision method can be done under local anesthesia. The clinician retrieves each vas deferens and cuts or seals them so they can no longer carry sperm to the outside world. For the no-scalpel method, the clinician navigates to the vasa deferentia within the scrotum and seals them (ACOG, March 2019).

EFFECTIVENESS

Female and male sterilization is over 99 percent effective. This method is often thought of as the standard of effectiveness. All other methods compare their own effectiveness to the results achieved by sterilization (Bedsider, 2019).

SIDE EFFECTS

The female sterilization surgery itself has minor expected complications, but the greatest risks are those that come with general anesthesia (such as damaging part of the airway). After the surgical procedure, females typically experience a bit of bleeding, bruising, and soreness that can last a few weeks. The risks include possible infection at the surgery site and ectopic pregnancy if the tubes somehow repair themselves. Again, these risks are extremely rare (Bedsider, 2019).

Both male sterilization procedures have quick recovery times with minimal risks or complications. It can take up to four months for this method to reach full effectiveness, and a clinician must recheck sperm levels to ensure effectiveness (ACOG, March 2019).

CONSIDERATIONS

In the present time, sterilization can work well for some people. In certain situations, medical professionals may be wary of assisting their patients in sterilization, especially young patients. Curtis, Mahllajee, and Peterson's systematic review from 2005 showed women under thirty who underwent sterilization were more likely to regret the decision and subsequently were more likely to request reversing this procedure. These research articles were mainly gathered from the late twentieth century, and perhaps regret came from not having full counseling efforts before making their decision.

Furthermore, the long-acting reversible contraceptives (LARCs) we have discussed so far only started gaining traction in the last three decades, and perhaps these women did not have access to the highly effective methods we have today. This could mean the sterilization option itself is useful in certain situations, but complete informed consent about sterilization's irreversibility and LARCs' high effectiveness is paramount.

On the other hand, it can be frustrating for some people with uteruses when they have considered the life they envision and in no capacity want to chance pregnancy. There are cases of people wanting to close that option permanently, and sometimes healthcare professionals deny them, fearing they "might change [their] mind" (Weissman, 2017) or "regret it" (Lalonde, 2018). These women feel frustrated by possible biases their doctors may impose, almost expecting them to have children. Instead, perhaps complete informed consent can be discussed and social expectations can be redefined.

COMMON MISCONCEPTIONS

Misconception: Sterilization can be reversed reliably, especially in males.

Although procedures designed to reverse sterilization surgeries exist, they cannot be relied on. Some surgeries can successfully reverse sterilization procedures but with varying degrees of effectiveness.

In van Seeters et al.'s 2017 systematic review of 10,689 women, pregnancy rates following female sterilization reversal were seen at 42–69 percent. The success of reversal was mostly dependent on age, whereas the type of surgical procedure used for reversal proved no increase in effectiveness. In-vitro fertilization where eggs are gathered from the ovaries instead may be a more viable option.

For studies in male sterilization, they typically search for successful rejoining of the vas deferens tubes (patency) and rates of pregnancy after surgery. In Herrel et al.'s 2015 systematic review of 6,633 patients, 89.4 percent of patients had their sperm return and 73 percent of them reported pregnancies after. Patency and pregnancy rates were more successful in individuals who underwent reversal less than ten years after sterilization.

In both these studies, pregnancy does not necessarily mean live births. The number of live births following sterilization reversal for both males and females is generally much lower than pregnancy rates.

Ultimately, both female and male sterilization is considered permanent.

With the advancements of birth control options today, even if there is a slight possibility pregnancy could be desired in the future, perhaps if situations or life changes, then other long-term reversible solutions exist with as much pregnancy prevention reliability as sterilization (IUDs and implant).

Misconception: Since sterilization is such a permanent and invasive procedure, it has always required thoroughly complete informed consent.

Margaret Sanger, the twentieth-century founder of Planned Parenthood and early pioneer of the birth control pill, went into reproductive rights activism because her good friend had a medical condition similar to Terri's. This friend died while giving birth, and all her doctor had done was advise her to sleep on the roof and avoid sexual intercourse with her husband. The frustration and despair fueled Sanger to ultimately fight for the widespread use of contraception (Wardell, 1980).

Similar to many other innovations in American history, contraception came as a double-edged sword with an intent to harm. The popular eugenics movement resulted in the forced sterilization of about 60,000 Americans (Reilly, 2015).

The eugenics movement sought to segregate "feeble-minded" people from the rest of the gene pool. Adam Cohen, in his book *Imbeciles,* reported people of color, "promiscuous" women, and poor people were disproportionately targeted. Institutionalization was the original mode of segregation, but that became a huge expense.

Government practices created avenues to sterilize these people without their consent, even telling them they would be undergoing an appendectomy instead. In 1927, the supreme court ruling *Buck v. Bell* made this procedure enforceable by states, and it has yet to be overturned even when it had the chance to in the 1940s. Once the US learned its own eugenics practices inspired terrifying Nazi sterilization practices, the US stopped this widespread practice (Sofair and Kaldjian, 2000).

However, the US continued to do so in some Black and Native American communities. For example, California prisons continued this practice on female inmates until 2010 (Chappell, 2013). In more recent events, certain ICE detention centers have been accused of performing compulsory sterilizations during the COVID-19 pandemic. From these horrific events, the medical community gained insights into this invasive surgical method (McEvoy, 2020).

Misconception: Hardly any men would be interested in additional male contraceptive options.

Most of the focus of this book revolves around female contraceptives as most available contraceptives are female targeted. However, over 80 percent of males claim pregnancy prevention is either their sole responsibility or shared equally between both partners (Friedman et al., 2019). With condoms and sterilization (vasectomy) as the only male contraceptive methods available, many men are left without a method to meet the demand.

In 2002, nine studies in nine different countries, with over one thousand male participants, showed that 55 percent of the men in the studies would try a new male contraceptive method if it were available. Of course, interest also depended on the simplicity of administration, such as a pill or infrequent injection (Heinemann et al., 2005).

In 2017, a random sample of fifteen-hundred reproductive age males was surveyed in the US. Through this research, they identified the US market has nineteen million potential users interested in new male contraceptive methods that would better fit their routine and relationship (Friedman et al., 2019).

In general, men and women agree contraception at its best should be the responsibility of both partners (Grady et al., 1996). Safety for both parties involved is a shared responsibility, just as preventing STIs is the responsibility of each individual. Although females claim they would have doubts in men using a contraceptive method properly, they are also quite interested in developing new contraceptives for men (Eberhardt, van Wersch, Meikle, 2009).

For the females who can't find a contraceptive method that suits their needs, what if their male partner could?

Many males like David would be happy to shoulder this responsibility for their female partners.

Misconception: Other than sterilization and male condoms, no other male contraceptive methods have been safely developed.

Male hormonal contraceptive methods have been developed and tested. Three main goals exist:

1. Decrease sperm count or azoospermia (normal level: 15-200 million, target level: less than 1 million)
2. Less than 1 percent of couples become pregnant after a year (over 99 percent effectiveness)
3. Return of fertility after discontinuing the method.

Several promising developments are currently under research. They are in varying stages of accomplishing the three goals above.

Testosterone Injections

A hormonal method has been developed that is an injection of synthetic testosterone. At baseline levels, when testosterone is produced, sperm is also produced. High levels of testosterone in the body tell the brain to actually *stop* producing testosterone. No more testosterone production, no more sperm production (Amory, 2020).

The WHO funded two studies for this method. In the first study, 271 men were given weekly shots, and 60 percent of them reached the targeted decreased sperm count. Furthermore, 119 of these men with decreased sperm count used it as their sole method of birth control for one year, and only one pregnancy occurred—over 99 percent effective (WHO, 1990).

In the second study, they tested not only azoospermic men but also severely low sperm count men that technically did not reach their target but were close (oligospermic). No pregnancies occurred in the azoospermic men. Eight in one hundred men caused pregnancy in the oligospermic group. Overall effectiveness reached 96.6 percent (WHO, 1996).

While the dosage of the synthetic testosterone still needs to be precisely determined, this provides valuable groundwork for future compositions.

Testosterone + Progestin Injections
Other injectable compositions have been made that add in progestin for more predictable decreased sperm counts. The addition of synthetic progesterone also helps tell the body to stop sperm production (Meriggiola and Bremner, 1997).

Synthetic Testosterone Implant + Progestin Injection
In general, men preferred not to go in frequently for weekly shots, and longer-term developments using implants have been created and tested (von Eckardstein et al., 2003). Testosterone implants plus progestin shots every few months have been shown to work effectively for preventing pregnancy (Turner et al., 2003).

Male Birth Control Pills

Several research institutions are highly invested in developing a novel male contraceptive pill. Two synthetic hormones have been created in pill form, DMAU (Thirumalai et al., 2019) and 11-βMNTDC (Attardi, 2011). These compositions contain both testosterone and progesterone activity to decrease sperm counts, but determining the precise and safe dosage is still in the works. While these drugs are still in the early phases of trials, men are highly interested in this simple and familiar mode of contraception.

Testosterone + Progesterone Topical Gel

Another promising male contraceptive is a daily applied gel containing both synthetic progesterone and testosterone called Nestorone/Testosterone. This drug's research is funded by the National Institutes of Health (NIH) and executed by the Population Council (the nonprofit global research organization that developed the copper IUD and the Mirena hormonal IUD). So far, its safety has been proven, and they are currently determining the proper dosage to achieve reduced sperm count and birth control effectiveness (Anawalt et al., 2019). The results are expected in 2022, and if all goes well, they can launch phase III trials for FDA approval.

Reversible "Vasectomy"

The final promising male contraceptive method we will touch upon is reversible inhibition of sperm under guidance (RISUG). This method was invented by Sujoy Guha in the Indian Institute of Technology and has been adopted in the US by Berkeley company Parsemus. For this method, a gel is injected into the vas deferens and physically blocks sperm release (similar to getting "tubes tied" or "snipped"). Then when the male would want to reverse this effect, they would get another injection to dissolve the gel and allow sperm to pass through, reinstating fertility (Parsemus, 2016).

This method is still in the very early stages of research development. Testing has yet to be administered on humans (Waller et al., 2017). Still, it provides a clever biologic strategy without relying on hormones. As we now know from looking at female options, hormonal methods tend to come with a wide array of side effects.

<u>Issues with Hormonal Male Contraceptives</u>
Three main issues are prevalent with hormonal male methods.

1. After starting these methods, it takes about two to three months to reach effective levels (similar to vasectomy). When stopping, it takes three to four months for fertility to return. Importantly, all these tested methods were shown to be predictably reversible. It just took longer than preferred for fertility to return.
2. Generally, these methods are not very effective yet. In the case of the female birth control pill, clinical trials were performed on women during loosely regulated times where researchers could show methods were highly effective at strikingly high doses, then taper back to safe dosages.
3. Users experienced many side effects.

<u>Hormonal Male Contraceptives Considerations</u>
The discussion around male birth control revolves around ethics. In general, when a medical intervention (like medication or surgical treatment) is suggested, the provider must determine the potential risks, benefits, and alternatives associated with treating a patient. If the proposed outcome would provide exceedingly more benefits than risks, then the intervention would be justified.

Females can use birth control to lower their chances of becoming pregnant. Pregnancy is associated with more serious health risks than birth control health risks. Exposing females to potential birth control side effects still lowers their overall risk of potentially worse pregnancy complications (CDC, 2021).

Males cannot become pregnant. Their risk of negative birth control side effects does not lower their overall health risk. In other words, these drugs would expose a male body to risks but do not provide the male body benefits. Their female partner's body would get the benefits.

This raises ethical questions and challenges our current social standards. Should we allow couples to make medical decisions for one another? Perhaps couples could mutually agree on male partners taking on minor birth control side effects since female partners inherently risk taking on major pregnancy consequences?

I feel we can draw parallels from other medical precedents. For example, if a person needs a kidney, another person can donate a kidney to them. The donor essentially gets nothing out of the arrangement that medically benefits them, and they undergo invasive surgery and come out with a fairly permanent outcome. The key here is mutual and thorough informed consent.

Perhaps taking on the contraceptive responsibility off a beloved partner could be seen in a similar way. With informed consent and a detailed explanation of the risks, benefits, and alternatives, maybe this could be a reality.

PUTTING IT ALL TOGETHER

Sterilization surgeries can provide peace of mind for people who know they are done having children and want to minimize that possibility as much as possible. The male vasectomy is less invasive, and recovery is simpler. The female sterilization process is also reliably effective but is more invasive and requires more healing time.

Lastly, like Terri and David, it could be beneficial to consider how a partner can share contraception responsibility and address their needs. Excitingly, medical advancements are in development that can hopefully make this a reality.

Until then, my hope is sexual partners will work together and share contraceptive responsibilities in ways that make sense for their relationship. Even if contraceptive methods that suit both partners' needs are not a reality yet, tools like open communication, recurring assessment, and curiosity are fundamental to relationships and health.

PART 3

CLOSING THOUGHTS

ZOOM OUT

As we hone in on the best contraceptive for ourselves and others, some people may feel their starting steps are pigeonholed. Rather than assume obstacles stem from one group, we can consider how responsibility is instead shared from a national scale to an individual scale.

GOVERNMENT RESPONSIBILITIES

Our nation's contraceptive climate has been reshaped considerably in recent events. The Affordable Care Act (ACA) imposed a federal contraceptive coverage guarantee. Under this law, women's preventive services, such as female-controlled contraceptive methods, STI testing, and appropriate counseling, are meant to be available to people without any out-of-pocket costs so long as they have some sort of insurance coverage, such as private health plans, self-insured plans, and government plans (Guttmacher, 2021).

The Contraceptive CHOICE Project proved no-cost contraception and LARC (long-acting reversible contraceptive) recommendations decreased abortion rates, decreased repeated abortions, and decreased teenage pregnancies (Secura, PhD, MPH et al., 2010).

When the ACA was first implemented, the use of contraception skyrocketed (Frost, Mueller, and Pleasure, 2021). Data from 2015–2019 shows coverage increased as the ACA provided coverage for contraception expanded, and people could choose to go to private practice clinics of their choice. Increased knowledge helped them desire and seek coverage, which is an important step in increasing preventive care. When financial barriers to preventive care arise, people use contraception less, which can end up creating costly consequences (like emergency room visits for untreated endometriosis or STIs).

The ACA was executed as a federal mandate, but states opted to place coverage restrictions and insurance coverage companies interpreted guidelines differently. This is what I have referred to often in this book as a patchwork of coverage across the US in terms of age restrictions, confidentiality, type of contraceptives covered, moral and religious objections, discrimination, and amount of contraceptives dispensed at once (Guttmacher, 2022).

This patchwork makes it difficult not only to explain in simple terms but also makes it difficult for many people in the US to understand their coverage. The answer to their coverage question is typically: "It depends." States, employers, and insurance companies impose limitations that affect coverage differently (Sonfield, February 2021). (For a starting point to find answers to coverage questions, see the Resource section.)

What does this coverage patchwork look like at the ground level? Some people across the country have difficulty attaining their contraceptive method of choice. Sometimes clinics are unable to serve more rural locations due to logistical issues (staffing, funding), while resources may be prohibited by agencies due to conflicting moral beliefs held by their officials.

As many people experienced, each political season can create a shift in access. Access to family planning services and women's preventive services has been on a political seesaw. (Keep in mind this is after eighteen years of Supreme Court rulings favoring informing women of all their options.) To this day, each time a different political party comes to power, access to contraception is switched. Individuals then must (re-)navigate their newly drawn medical rights in this complex healthcare bureaucracy (Ahmed, 2020).

"This is something central to a woman's life, to her dignity. It's a decision that she must make for herself. And when government controls that decision for her, she's being treated as less than a fully adult human responsible for her own choices. While these decisions continue to decide for us what happens to our bodies, we are not truly treated as respectable beings."

—JUSTICE RUTH BADER GINSBURG

Since there is not necessarily a uniform coverage standard across the US, answering questions about an individual's coverage is complicated. What can we do about this?

Maybe we can forge a more permanent and consistent path to coverage that would not leave so many women at a loss once the next term comes around. Hopefully, they would not have to experience the shock of finding out their reliable contraceptive method is no longer available to them.

***

As we have seen through various stories, people prefer contraceptives that work well for their lifestyles. This allows them to consistently use contraception and avoid unwanted side effects. Ultimately, to help people with coverage, the federal government can continue to uphold its responsibility to its people and fully enact comprehensive contraceptive coverage.

During the Trump administration, legislation was passed allowing employers to avoid covering contraception on moral or religious grounds (Millhiser, 2020). Furthermore, the Trump administration created limitations to Title X funding, which burdened many contraceptive resource clinics. These clinics provide a wide array of women's preventive services, typically in one visit (Guttmacher, 2021). In general, people of lower socio-economic status and people of color predominantly attain care at these clinics.

With essentially 50 percent of Title X resources under fire due to lack of funding, hundreds of thousands of people using contraception have been in a frenzy seeking to receive healthcare (Zolna, Finn, and Frost, 2020). Instead, funding has been funneled to organizations that have different goals, many times not providing contraceptive resources due to moral objections (Sonfield, 2019). Reproductive age people without insurance increased during the Trump administration as well (Sonfield, April 2021). The full scope of the impact of the Trump administration is currently under review, but it will likely take several months to years for clinics and individuals to recover.

Organizations have been reported to create loopholes that prevent people from getting their method of choice covered. In a Kaiser Family Foundation 2020 survey, they found 18 percent of privately insured people are not getting the contraceptive methods they want, and 21 percent are still paying out-of-pocket costs. This may be due to several factors. Insurance companies are incentivized like any other company to keep their costs low. If they have to pay premium costs when patients want an expensive birth control pill, for example, they tend to deny those requests if a cheaper alternative exists.

Additionally, some agencies have denied coverage stating a contraceptive is denied coverage as it exists in a similar form. In other words, a patient may prefer to use the patch, but the specific progestin and ratio of progestin-estrogen may be found in a cheaper pill form. Coverage has been denied on grounds those are the same, but we have learned they are different for several reasons.

Medical providers can help their patients appeal to their insurance companies, especially when specific contraceptives are needed for specific medical concerns (Cunningham, 2013). Also, the National Women's Law Center has hotline and email resources that help inform people of their contraceptive costs rights and helps them get coverage (see the Resources section for more information).

Some people have schedule limitations that do not allow them to go places during regular business hours. For those that require an in-person doctor visit to get a prescription or those that may find it difficult to go to their pharmacy, it may be difficult to use contraception as regularly as they would like. Over-the-counter methods like sponges and spermicides are only covered with a prescription. The federal government can extend coverage for patients without a prescription.

Perhaps opening a new channel to have more methods available over the counter and making it possible to allow patients to receive a twelve-month supply of their contraceptive method of choice would help increase consistent use (Guttmacher, 2021). Some high-quality studies showed patients were more likely to continue using their methods consistently—decreasing their rates of abortions—when they were given more than a seven-month or even one-year supply of birth control pills at once (Foster et al., 2011).

We need the federal government to align its goals with the recommendations of the scientific and medical community. To do this, they can continue to uphold their ACA mandates, checking their regulations are followed according to the standards they have outlined. They can look to eliminate barriers that keep people from attaining comprehensive care. As new loopholes are used, they can continue to clarify their message and stand firm in their decision to prioritize the health of all people.

EDUCATION SYSTEM RESPONSIBILITIES

Just as a patchwork of contraceptive access exists, a patchwork of contraceptive education exists. Only thirty-nine states and the District of Columbia require general sexual education and/or HIV education, and only twenty of these states require content about contraception (Guttmacher Institute: Sex and HIV Education, 2022).

Surprisingly, even with surmised stereotypical fear tactics, students are still not consistently familiar with how to prevent HIV/STIs or pregnancy. In 2014, the CDC's School Health Profiles assessed national trends in schools regarding health education. In the sexual education category, they found only 45.5 percent of high schools taught the sixteen recommended HIV, STD, and pregnancy prevention topics, such as preventive services, sexual behavior communication, limiting sexual partners, relationship development, goal setting and decision-making, and finding accurate information. When it came to specific knowledge of contraceptive methods, only 43 percent of schools taught about them.

Furthermore, we are noticing an overall decline in teens receiving formal sex education in schools while not increasing in their knowledge from their parents. As for contraception knowledge, researchers found the number of teens who received formal education on contraceptives before their first sex experience dropped (in females from 62 to 57 and in males from 52 to 43 percent) from 2006–2010 to 2011–2013 (Lindberg, PhD, Maddow-Zimet, Boonstra, MA, 2016).

Perhaps this could be due to teens resorting to finding their information online? If that is the case, this may be worrisome as we cannot guarantee where their information comes from nor its medical accuracy.

Although we cannot draw specific conclusions about why we are noticing these declining trends in sexual education, we can continue to look at ways we can improve current sex education programs and hopefully inspire educators to revive them. Many of my friends and colleagues remember their sexual education classes as awkward, sex-negative, and unsuccessful. They were not standardized, and they tended to focus on negative outcomes and abstinence. Young people may receive a message that contradicts their desires and discredit the information presented in the class as a whole.

Young people tend to underestimate issues like their own fertility, and contraception knowledge tends to be very limited. We need an invested coalition of teachers willing to provide comprehensive sexuality education. This would include collaborating with students on topics of interest and prioritizing accordingly. Should students need resources in the future, this education would hopefully equip students with accurate health information and language to communicate their sexuality needs.

Part of this initiation requires addressing the discomfort often felt by students and teachers surrounding sex education. SIECUS, the leading organization on sexual education, suggests discussing relationships and sexuality topics in simpler, destigmatizing ways in elementary and middle school to help normalize high school level classes and discussions (SIECUS, 2004). Classes can also share information using strategies in this book, highlighting stories and showing students these topics are applicable to them.

Learning how these methods may feel for other users sheds light on how it could feel for them too. The more familiar methods are, the more approachable. The more approachable, the more accessible they will have to become. As demand grows, health organizations, practitioners, and clinics will have to find ways to meet these demands. Education shows us and pushes us to create the changes we need to overcome contraceptive deficits.

SCIENTIFIC COMMUNITY RESPONSIBILITIES
Over 30 percent of women using reversible contraceptives switched methods within two years. One in ten of

these women chose to not use contraception altogether. This likely has to do with changing life circumstances, but they also disclosed they were not planning to have a pregnancy at this time (Grady, Billy, and Klepinger, 2002). More likely, researchers believe this may stem from dis-satisfaction with methods available, possibly from the aforementioned access issues, unmet expectations, or the inability of current methods to meet their goals.

Many contraceptive needs are not met globally, let alone on an individual level. We have to weigh the risks and benefits when deciding between options. Reliable protec-tion can give people enormous relief. Exchanging severe negative period symptoms with milder contraceptive side effects may be an overall positive trade-off. This is also not to say we should be complacent with the methods we have and accept their side effects. We can continue pushing the boundaries of our current contraceptives, improving their capabilities.

Perhaps we can also improve contraceptive experiences by supporting companies gathering data to better predict side effects individuals may experience and determine more tolerable methods. Perhaps there could be an avenue for personalized medicine approaches.

***

We have discussed at length the safety of the birth con-trol pill and some of the issues surrounding access. There is a movement now to get a safe, low-dose birth control pill over the counter. This would provide people with more discretion and more accessibility in case they are unable to receive care from a health clinic or a doctor.

Also, only two methods provide both birth control and STI prevention, the internal condom and the external condom. The research community can also devote resources to creating more STI prevention options. Excitingly, a new ring (NIH, 2020) and a new diaphragm method (Bedsider, 2015) have been formulated to help protect against HIV. These methods work as described in previous chapters but have an extra layer of drug protection built in. These added drugs help fight against HIV locally to stop an infection from taking hold. More research is needed to verify the effectiveness of pregnancy prevention as well as HIV prevention, but the idea is promising and can be created and distributed relatively inexpensively.

A significant population of men want to help share contraceptive responsibility with their female partners more tangibly. We can continue creating new developments for them. New hormonal male contraceptive methods have been developed and are undergoing testing. Although it will still take more time for them to safely come to market, it is reassuring knowing companies are invested in making this a reality.

Overall, there is still a need to improve existing methods and develop new reliable female and male non-hormonal and hormonal methods with fewer side effects.

***

Responsibility over a person's contraceptive experience is often contested. Government regulations may impose restrictions, education may not be readily accessible, and an individual's available resources may not address their needs. Perhaps we can all consider how our decisions and jurisdictions affect those around us.

ZOOM IN

Throughout this book, we have learned the importance of evaluating our own health, discerning which lessons serve us amid our contraceptive climate. We can consider how our support system can share responsibilities to help us understand our bodies.

With support, we can navigate contraception together. With reflection, we can initiate ownership and familiarity with our bodies.

MEDICAL PROVIDER RESPONSIBILITIES

Medical providers play a huge role in educating the public. In general, we rightly celebrate and thank our medical providers for their selfless and demanding work. Many medical facilities across the US have limited resources, and providers have limited time to work with patients. Commonly, providers prioritize the well-being of their patients or else they would not be in this field.

Medical providers, too, can continue to shape the current contraceptive climate. The major health professional organizations, such as the American College of Obstetrics and Gynecology and the Centers for Disease Control, independently and unanimously recommend providers counsel patients regardless of sexual activity on the full range of contraceptive options available (including emergency contraception). Additionally, they recommend health professionals provide one or more of the methods on-site if possible (WPSI, 2017).

Several high-quality and large-scale research articles demonstrate the ways medical provider counseling makes a huge impact. Counseling was shown to help patients use their contraceptive methods more consistently when they were told other medications they were taking would have negative effects on a potential embryo or fetus (Schwarz et al., 2012). Additionally, primary care providers can help counsel patients to use highly effective LARC methods as contraception with detailed evaluation and discussion (Lee et al., 2011). This could help patients consistently reduce their reproductive health issues. During family planning visits, providers can help lower pregnancy rates for interested patients using adequate counseling on highly effective methods like LARCs (Harper et al., 2015).

Finally, medical providers can continue being aware of ways people may have misconceived notions about contraception. They can continue learning, educating and counseling, listening, advocating for patients, and aligning recommendations to the most current research available. Providers *can* help motivate patients to stay consistent with their contraception and help them improve their reproductive health.

PERSONAL COMMUNITY RESPONSIBILITIES

For some parents, discussing sexuality with their child can feel daunting. Although it can feel difficult for some, early conversations on contraception can dissuade them from engaging in risky sexual behaviors and instead stay safe and healthy. Sex education experts agree parents and guardians, in an ideal scenario, would be primarily responsible for leading sexuality discussions with their children.

In a national poll conducted by Planned Parenthood of over 1,663 pairs of parents, over 90 percent agree sex education is important in middle school and high school. Over 20 percent of parents had never spoken with their fifteen- to twenty-year-old about "strategies for saying no to sex, birth control methods, or where to get accurate sexual health information," while over 30 percent never spoke about "where to get reproductive health care services."

This shows a separation of the value in these discussions from its implementation. Why? Some parents and children may feel too embarrassed, parents may not know when to properly time these situations, parents may default to relying on other community members, and parents may feel their knowledge is lacking. However, that same Planned Parenthood poll shows both parents and children did not think these were major contributors.

We may just have to default to recognizing that every situation is different and think of strategies that can help us feel prepared to start or navigate these conversations when they do come up. A helpful strategy can be talking to a child a little at a time rather than waiting for an arbitrary time for "the talk." This helps normalize their experience rather than keeping certain topics or words as shameful or taboo (PPFA, 2022).

In general, it can be helpful for parents or guardians to stay curious and leave lines of communication open with their young person. It can be a huge relief to the young person to know their parent or guardian can be trusted for information and support without judgment. Resources can be found for how parents can address specific topics in age-appropriate terms online (see the Resources section for some helpful links).

As many stories highlighted in previous chapters have shown, friends and other close personal connections are often involved in conversations about sexual health and contraception. If a person has questions about contraception, maybe their friend does too. It could be helpful to identify trusted people to learn from. Maybe contraceptive knowledge can be built as a network, helping each person determine places to find reliable resources and services.

PARTNER RESPONSIBILITIES

Many partners care about the other's well-being. Partnerships tend to have responsibilities to one another in some way. Perhaps we can consider and reconsider additional ways to help and support a partner with contraception.

Male partners with female partners who house most of the contraceptive responsibility can perhaps share in the financial burden. Taking advantage of coverage may help their partner cover costs, such as using funds from a health account (FSA, HSA, HRA) to purchase condoms.

For all partners, it could be worthwhile to normalize talking about contraception early in the relationship in order to find ways to support one another and stay safe. Maybe one can plan ahead and already prepare (properly handled) condoms. Also, getting tested regularly helps alleviate some STI concerns, especially when people may have multiple partners.

Perhaps all partners can be open to trying new methods too. When both people in a partnership feel comfortable, it may be more of a benefit than any slight discomfort from a contraceptive method (like feeling a cervical cap or ring during sex). After adjusting to the feeling of a new method, partners may even come to enjoy them or not even notice them.

Perhaps these conversations can lead to both people learning more about the contraceptive method of choice. This may help them both evaluate how it feels, learn how to communicate it, and determine if any support is needed. Maybe even something as simple as helping partners pick up the method from a convenience store or pharmacy would be a huge help.

Overall, clear communication with partners can bring them into our support system and make the contraception journey less daunting and more assuring.

RESPONSIBILITY TO OURSELVES

Lastly, we are our own best advocates. We owe it to ourselves to find a method that fits our lifestyle without settling for subpar outcomes. After looking at the different options available, we have to return to our experience. What is the main reason for choosing contraception—painful periods, pregnancy prevention, a combination? For pregnancy prevention, what level of effectiveness is important? Over 99 percent, 87–93 percent, at least some? Is STI prevention needed? Is it important to have a more familiar mode like a pill or shot? How regularly could a regimen be kept—daily, weekly, monthly, yearly?

With these considerations in mind, many people can find a contraceptive that fits them and their lifestyle safely. For some, they use a method (or combination of methods) for years and years with no problems and no noticeable changes. Some have to go on a journey to find this fit, and it may take several months of trial and error before their hormones acclimate successfully. Some go off birth control when life changes, and sometimes they return to it.

I believe it is possible to find a contraceptive that fits our values, makes our bodies feel good, and works with our cultural traditions. This book provides the first step in empathizing with our own and others' experiences.

We can now learn more about ourselves and develop the language to communicate our needs.

Drug or medical device companies are not aware of the unintended consequences their products have until others experience them. Sharing feedback is useful for improving products.

We have an important responsibility to ourselves to stay safe and manage our health. Working with our doctors, we need to regularly partake in preventive tools and services (like STI testing and PAP smears).

Finding the courage and opportunities to share our story helps not only to reinforce lessons but also helps others continually look for ways to improve their experience. Listening to stories and even seeking them out helps remove embarrassing stigmas and normalizes sexuality as a part of the human experience.

***

We can continue the contraceptive dialogue by involving partners and healthcare providers, advocating for more options and development, forming healthy relationships, sharing our stories, and supporting one another in our journeys.

Maybe now, after reading this book, we can all look through a new lens of truth with reformed conceptions. We can leap from this foundational stepping stone, continue to expand our own knowledge, and share what we have learned and experienced with others. Sexual health and biological sciences do not have to be disjointed or disheartening.

Our bodies can feel whole; we all deserve the opportunity to thrive and feel our best.

RESOURCES

For information on specific state policies on contraception coverage and access as well as minor access, anonymity, consent laws, check out the Guttmacher Institute's webpage.

For more in-depth analyses of contraceptive history, must-reads are Linda Gordon's book, *The Moral Property of Women: A History of Birth Control Politics in America,* and Angela Tone's book, *Devices and Desires: A History of Contraceptives in America.*

For insurance coverage information regarding a specific situation, submit a request online or call the National Women's Law Center (NWLC), or even call a local Planned Parenthood.

For additional information on fertility awareness-based methods, check out Power to Decide's website Bedsider for a list of various tracking methods.

To find government 340B Drug Pricing Program clinics in a specific location, go through the Health Resources and

Services Administration website and input the city and state (https://340bopais.hrsa.gov/searchlanding).

For help with age-appropriate sex and contraception conversations, find helpful tips on Planned Parenthood's webpage.

ACKNOWLEDGEMENTS

Thank you, Mom. I constantly rely on your guidance. Thank you for giving me a greater life than I could have imagined. Thank you for all you have endured to give me a beautiful life of joy and gratitude. Thank you for always wanting the best for me and telling me when I might be settling. Thank you for your constant reaffirmations of love.

Thank you, Dad. I am so thankful for your magical gift of storytelling. I aspire to have your delivery and approachability. You are the life of the party and always full of surprises. Your shenanigans of love uplift my days. Thank you for showing me how it's possible to build and grow at all stages of life. Thank you for being such a good, generous, and giving man.

Thank you, Miko, Marcus, and Michael, for believing in me and bringing me encouragement when I need it most. Thank you for being proud of me regardless of my accomplishments. Thank you for constantly revolutionizing my views of family and society. You are so important to me. I strive to be an example and role model for you, although you inspire me and influence me more than you know.

Thank you, Teddy Cho, for seeing me beyond what I say or do. Thank you for your talented creative assistance. Thank you for making this book a reality when I was at my worst and when I truly thought I could not go on. Thank you for providing me with the security to succeed in my endeavors, and thank you for always believing in me, encouraging me, and growing me.

Thank you, Joyce Yang, for being such a present friend in this strange world of adulthood. Thank you for inspiring me to impact the world for the better and teaching me how to consider alternative perspectives. Thank you for challenging me to question the world around me; thank you for spending the time to help me make this book as great as it could be. I am so grateful and truly cherish our multidimensional friendship that is fun, divinely oriented, and so much more.

Thank you, Alex Nguyen, for being an essential part of forming my grit and compassion. Thank you for leading others in your thoughtfulness and challenging us to all be better friends and humans. Thank you for sound-boarding and entertaining my strangest thoughts. Thank you for hearing the things I need to say. Thank you for saying the things I need to hear.

Thank you to Aislyn Gilbert for your cheerful encouragement, Tasslyn Magnusson for helping me create a detailed and constructive vision, Michelle Pollack for your confidence in directing a clear path to my message, Eric Koester and the rest of the team at Creator Institute and New Degree Press for upholding your mission of giving a voice to authors. Thank you for mapping out pitfalls and creating a path toward success.

Thank you to all who provided crucial feedback during my writing process, helping me shape this book's message and flow. Thank you to all my friends and interviewees who opened up and shared their stories with me and helped me grasp a deeper understanding of the contraceptive climate. Thank you for all you do to help improve reproductive rights and access all over the globe.

Finally, thank you to my cherished and beloved family, friends, and supporters. Thank you for receiving my ideas and believing in my endeavors. Thank you for the ways you have shown up and been present in my life. Your constant accountability in my well-being and progress has made this book a reality. A special thank you to everyone who pre-ordered a copy of my book and supported my prelaunch campaign. Thank you for being my community:

Aaron Sulaeman	Andrew Occiano
Abi K	Angelli Chua
Adri Martinez	Annie Zhu
Alex Des Pres	Astrude Escasa
Alex Nguyen	Barbara Galera, DDS
Alex Rauchle	Bernadette Lingat
Alice Hu	Carrie Balthrop
Alice Tong	Choua Her
Amy Ng	Chris Lee

Cody Tran
Eric Koester
Erika Lee
Evan Yao
Frank L
Grace Chung
Hazel Velasco
Heather L
Isabel Kuo
Isabella Benavente
Janeen Ibarreta
Jasmine Yee
Jennifer Guo
Jenny Kot
Jenny Ng
Jessica Drouin
Jonathan Lian
Johnny Occiano-Nilsen
Joyce Yang
Julia Lim
Julie Anne Wear
Justin Li
Katelyn Fischer
Katherine Diep
Kelly Nguyen
Kristine Torres
Lavern Zhang
Lukas Pham
Ma Htet Poe
Mark Berbano
Matthew Mizono
Mega Patel
Megan Fong
Melinda Wik
Michelle Kwon
Millie Benavente
Miriam Pasimio
MyHanh Duong
Natalie Okuhara
Patrick Ngo
Patrick Trillo
Ren Urena
Ryan Tran
Ryan Wong
Salley Park
Samantha Mohan
Sarah Ouyang
Serin Lee
Shannon Austria
Sharon Fang
Shira Chu
Stephanie Do
Teddy Cho
William Barbeau

APPENDIX

INTRODUCTION

Barot, Sneha. "The Benefits of Investing in International Family Planning—and the Price of Slashing Funding." *Guttmacher Policy Review* 20 (August 2017). https://www.guttmacher.org/gpr/2017/08/benefits-investing-international-family-planning-and-price-slashing-funding.

CDC U.S. Department of Health & Human Services. "Contraception." 2022. https://www.cdc.gov/reproductivehealth/contraception/index.htm.

Dreweke, Joerg. "Promiscuity Propaganda: Access to Information and Services Does Not Lead to Increases in Sexual Activity." *Guttmacher Policy Review*, Volume 22 (June 11, 2019): 29-36. https://www.guttmacher.org/gpr/2019/06/promiscuity-propaganda-access-information-and-services-does-not-lead-increases-sexual.

Frost, Jennifer, Susheela Singh, Lawrence B. Finer. "U.S. Women's One-Year Contraceptive Use Patterns, 2004." March 8, 2007. https://doi.org/10.1363/3904807.

Guttmacher Institute. "Sex and HIV Education." January 1, 2022. https://www.guttmacher.org/state-policy/explore/sex-and-hiv-education.

Guttmacher Institute. "Contraceptive Use in the United States by Demographics." May 2021. https://www.guttmacher.org/fact-sheet/contraceptive-use-united-states.

Jones, Rachel K. "Reported contraceptive use in the month of becoming pregnant among U.S. abortion patients in 2000 and 2014." *Contraception* 97, no. 4 (April 2018): 309-312. https://doi.org/10.1016/j.contraception.2017.12.018.

Kaye, K., Suellentrop, K., and Sloup, C. (2009). *The Fog Zone: How Misperceptions, Magical Thinking, and Ambivalence Put Young Adults at Risk for Unplanned Pregnancy*. Washington, DC: Power to Decide (formerly The National Campaign to Prevent Teen and Unplanned Pregnancy). https://powertodecide.org/what-we-do/information/resource-library/fog-zone.

Schroeder, EdD, MSW, Elizabeth, Eva Goldfarb, PhD, Nora Gelperin, MEd. Advocates for Youth. "Rights, Respect, Responsibility. A K-12 Sexuality Education Curriculum. Teacher's Guide." 2022. https://advocatesforyouth.org/wp-content/uploads/3rscurric/teachers-guide.pdf.

Sully, Elizabeth, Ann Biddlecom, Jacqueline E. Darroch, Taylor Riley, Lori S. Ashford, Naomi Lince-Deroche, Lauren Firestein and Rachel Murro. Guttmacher Institute. "Adding It Up: Investing in Sexual and Reproductive Health 2019." July 2020. https://www.guttmacher.org/report/adding-it-upinvesting-in-sexual-reproductive-health-2019.

World Health Organization. "Contraception Evidence Brief: Contraception enables people to make informed choices about their sexual and reproductive health." Human Reproduction Programme. 2019. https://apps.who.int/iris/bitstream/handle/10665/329884/WHO-RHR-19.18-eng.pdf?ua=1.

KEY TERMS AND DEFINITIONS

American Pregnancy Association. "Spotting During Pregnancy." 2021. https://americanpregnancy.org/healthy-pregnancy/pregnancy-concerns/spotting-during-pregnancy/.

Azziz, Ricardo, Enrico Carmina, ZiJiang Chen, Andrea Dunaif, Joop S. E. Laven, Richard S. Legro, Daria Lizneva, Barbara Natterson-Horowtiz, Helena J. Teede, and Bulent O. Yildiz. "Polycystic ovary syndrome." *Nature Reviews Disease Primers* 2, no. 16057 (August 11, 2016). DOI: 10.1038/nrdp.2016.57.

Blackman, Stuart. "Do any non-human animals menstruate?" *BBC Wildlife*, September 1, 2017. https://www.discoverwildlife.com/animal-facts/do-any-non-human-animals-menstruate/.

Edwards, Michael, and Ahmet S. Can. *Progestin*. Treasure Island: StatPearls Publishing LLC, September 22, 2021. https://www.ncbi.nlm.nih.gov/books/NBK563211/.

French, MD, Valerie. "What You Should Know About Breakthrough Bleeding With Birth Control." Last updated January 2021. https://www.acog.org/womens-health/experts-and-stories/the-latest/what-you-should-know-about-breakthrough-bleeding-with-birth-control#:~:text=Breakthrough%20bleeding%20rarely%20signals%20a,your%20ob%2Dgyn%20can%20help.&text=Breakthrough%20bleeding%20is%20a%20common,some%20women%20have%20heavier%20bleeding.

Kimmel, Michael S. *The Gendered Society,* New York: Oxford University Press, 2000.

Office on Women's Health in the Office of the Assistant Secretary for Health at the U.S. Department of Health and Human Services. "Sexually transmitted infections." June 11, 2019. https://www.womenshealth.gov/a-z-topics/sexually-transmitted-infections#:~:text=An%20STI%20is%20an%20infection,some%20STIs%20cannot%20be%20cured.

Office on Women's Health in the Office of the Assistant Secretary for Health at the U.S. Department of Health and Human Services. "Your menstrual cycle." March 16, 2018. https://www.womenshealth.gov/menstrual-cycle/your-menstrual-cycle.

Ray, DNP, Laurie. "What is the menstrual cycle?" Clue by Biowink GmbH, November 7, 2021. https://helloclue.com/articles/cycle-a-z/the-menstrual-cycle-more-than-just-the-period.

Rodriguez, MD, Maria Isabel. "Is it really okay to skip periods?" Bedsider. Last updated May 20, 2015. https://www.bedsider.org/features/75-is-it-really-okay-to-skip-periods.

HISTORY

Ballentine, Carol. "Sulfanilamide Disaster. Taste of Raspberries, Taste of Death: The 1937 Elixir Sulfanilamide Incident." *FDA Consumer,* June 1981. https://www.fda.gov/files/about%20fda/published/The-Sulfanilamide-Disaster.pdf.

Bill and Melinda Gates Foundation. "Family Planning." 1991-2022. https://www.gatesfoundation.org/our-work/programs/global-development/family-planning.

Engelman, Peter. *A History of* the *Birth Control Movement.* Santa Barbara, Praeger: 2011.

Gordon, Linda. *The Moral Property of Women.* 3rd ed. Champaign, University of Illinois Press: 2002.

Guttmacher Institute. "Contraceptive Use in the United States by Demographics." May 2021. https://www.guttmacher.org/fact-sheet/contraceptive-use-united-states.

Hubacher, David. "The Checkered History and Bright Future of Intrauterine Contraception in the United States." *Perspectives on Sexual and Reproductive Health* 34, no. 2 (March 1, 2002): 98-103. https://doi.org/10.1363/3409802.

Independence Hall Association in Philadelphia. "Victorian Values in a New Age." Accessed January 31, 2022. https://www.ushistory.org/us/39d.asp.

Jensen, Joan M. "The Evolution of Margaret Sanger's 'Family Limitation' Pamphlet, 1914-1921." *Signs* 6, no. 3 (1981): 548-657. https://www.jstor.org/stable/3173773.

Lopez, Laureen M, Shanthi Ramesh, Mario Chen, Alison Edelman, Conrad Otterness, James Trussell, Frans M Helmerhorst. "Progestin-only contraceptives: effects on weight." Cochrane Database of Systematic Reviews 8, no. CD008815 (2016). doi: 10.1002/14651858.CD008815.pub4.

Michals, PhD, Debra. "Margaret Sanger (1879-1966)." National Women's History Museum. 2017. https://www.womenshistory.org/education-resources/biographies/margaret-sanger.

Planned Parenthood Federation of America, Inc. "Our History." Accessed February 14, 2022. https://www.plannedparenthood.org/about-us/who-we-are/our-history.

Planned Parenthood Federation of America, Inc. "The Birth Control Pill: A History." Last updated June 2015. https://www.plannedparenthood.org/files/1514/3518/7100/Pill_History_FactSheet.pdf.

Price, Michael E., Nicholas Pound, and Isabel M. Scott. "Female Economic Dependence and the Morality of Promiscuity." *Archives of Sexual Behavior.* 43, 1289–1301 (2014). https://doi.org/10.1007/s10508-014-0320-4.

Roosevelt, Theodore. Theodore Roosevelt to Charles Davenport. "Society should not permit degenerates to reproduce their kind." *The Outlook,* January 3, 1913. American Philosophical Society. https://eugenics.us/letter-by-theodore-roosevelt-to-charles-davenport-society-should-not-permit-degenerates-to-reproduce-their-kind/176.htm.

Tone, Angela. *Devices and Desires: A History of Contraceptives in America.* New York, Hill and Wang A division of Farrar, Straus, and Giroux: 2001.

U.S. Food and Drug Administration. "Part I: The 1906 Food and Drugs Act and Its Enforcement." Last modified April 24, 2019. https://www.fda.gov/about-fda/changes-science-law-and-regulatory-authorities/part-i-1906-food-and-drugs-act-and-its-enforcement.

U.S. Food and Drug Administration. "Part II: 1938, Food, Drug, Cosmetic Act." Last modified November 27, 2018. https://www.fda.gov/about-fda/changes-science-law-and-regulatory-authorities/part-ii-1938-food-drug-cosmetic-act.

U.S. Food and Drug Administration. "Part III: Drugs and Foods Under the 1938 Act and Its Amendments." Last modified February 1, 2018. https://www.fda.gov/about-fda/changes-science-law-and-regulatory-authorities/part-iii-drugs-and-foods-under-1938-act-and-its-amendments.

THE PILL

American Migraine Foundation. "Understanding Migraine with Aura." Last updated July 6, 2017. https://americanmigrainefoundation.org/resource-library/understanding-migraine-aura/.

Breastcancer.org. "Is There a Link Between Birth Control Pills and Higher Breast Cancer Risk?" Last updated August 4, 2014. https://www.breastcancer.org/research-news/study-

questions-birth-control-and-risk#:~:text=If%20you've%20
been%20diagnosed,cancer%20coming%20back%20(recur-
rence).

Cooper, Danielle and Heba Mahdy. "Oral Contraceptive Pills."
Treasure Island: StatPearls Publishing LLC. December 16,
2021. https://www.ncbi.nlm.nih.gov/books/NBK430882/.

Darney, PD. "The androgenicity of progestins." *American
Journal of Medicine* 1A, (1995): 104-110. DOI: 10.1016/s0002-
9343(99)80067-9.

Edlow, MD, MSc, Andrea and Deborah Bartz, MD, MPH. "Hormonal Contraceptive Options for Women With Headache:
A Review of the Evidence." *Reviews in Obstetrics and Gynecology* 3, no. 2 (2010): 55-65. https://www.ncbi.nlm.nih.gov/pmc/
articles/PMC2938905/.

French, MD, Valerie. "A quick guide to skipping periods
with birth control." *Bedsider.* September 18, 2013. https://
powertodecide.org/sexual-healthyour-sexual-healthar-
ticles-about-healthy-sex-life/quick-guide-skipping-peri-
ods-birth#:~:text=Answer%3A%20Monophasic%20pills%20
cause%20less,needed%20to%20skip%20your%20period.

Girum, Tadele and Abebaw Wasie. "Return of fertility after
discontinuation of contraception: a systematic review and
meta-analysis." *Contraception and Reproductive Medicine* 3, no.
9 (July 23, 2018). doi: 10.1186/s40834-018-0064-y.

Jackson, MD, Andrea. "Late, late, for a very important pill?" *Bedsider.* Last updated June 23, 2016. https://www.bedsider.org/features/153-late-late-for-a-very-important-pill.

Jones, EE. "Androgenic effects of oral contraceptives: implications for patient compliance." *American Journal of Medicine* 1A (1995): 116-119. doi: 10.1016/s0002-9343(99)80069-2.

Karas, Jay, dir. *Ali Wong Baby Cobra.* May 5, 2016. Burbank, CA: Comedy Dynamics and New Wave Entertainment. Aired on Netflix.

Lewis, Carolin A, Ann-Christin S Kimmig, Rachel G Zsido, Alexander Jank, Birgit Derntl, Julia Sacher. "Effects of Hormonal Contraceptives on Mood: A Focus on Emotion Recognition and Reactivity, Reward Processing, and Stress Response." *Current Psychiatry Reports* 21, no. 11 (2019). doi:10.1007/s11920-019-1095-z.

Lopez, Laureen M, Shanthi Ramesh, Mario Chen, Alison Edelman, Conrad Otterness, James Trussell, Frans M Helmerhorst. "Progestin-only contraceptives: effects on weight." Cochrane Database of Systematic Reviews 8, no. CD008815 (2016). doi: 10.1002/14651858.CD008815.pub4.

Mona, Breanna, Kimberly Holland, Stacy A. Henigsman, DO. "Birth Control Brands: How to Choose What's Right for You." Healthline. Last updated December 7, 2021. https://www.healthline.com/health/birth-control/birth-control-pill-brands#combination-pills.

National Cancer Institute at the National Institutes of Health. "Oral Contraceptives and Cancer Risk." Last updated February 22, 2018. https://www.cancer.gov/about-cancer/causes-prevention/risk/hormones/oral-contraceptives-fact-sheet#:~:text=Naturally%20occurring%20estrogen%20and%20progesterone,potentially%20also%20increase%20cancer%20risk.

Office on Women's Health in the Office of the Assistant Secretary for Health at the U.S. Department of Health and Human Services. "Birth control methods." Last updated February 14, 2019. https://www.womenshealth.gov/a-z-topics/birth-control-methods.

Planned Parenthood Federation of America Inc. "Birth Control Pill." 2005. https://www.plannedparenthood.org/learn/birth-control/birth-control-pill.

Power to Decide. "Bedsider." 2019. https://www.bedsider.org/birth-control/the_pill.

Robakis, Thalia, Katherine E Williams, Lexi Nutkiewicz, Natalię L Rasgon. "Hormonal Contraceptives and Mood: Review of the Literature and Implications for Future Research." *Current Psychiatry Reports* 21, no. 7: 57. doi: 10.1007/s11920-019-1034-z.

Roland, James, and Alan Carter PharmD. "Is the Last Week of Birth Control Pills Necessary?" Healthline. May 11, 2019. https://www.healthline.com/health/birth-control/last-week-of-birth-control-pills#the-basics.

SEER Training Modules. "Characteristics of Hormones." U. S. National Institutes of Health, National Cancer Institute. Last accessed February 18, 2022. https://training.seer.cancer.gov/anatomy/endocrine/hormones.html.

Silver, Natalie and Debra Rose Wilson, Ph.D., MSN, R.N., IBCLC, AHN-BC, CHT. "Using Birth Control to Improve Acne." Healthline. Last updated January 28, 2022. https://www.healthline.com/health/best-birth-control-for-acne#pills-approved-for-acne.

Taylor, Attia. "How long does it take for the pill to become effective?" Planned Parenthood Federation of America Inc. April 29, 2020. https://www.plannedparenthood.org/learn/teens/ask-experts/how-long-does-it-take-for-the-pill-to-become-effective.

Weisburg, Edith and Ian S. Fraser. "Contraception and endometriosis: challenges, efficacy, and therapeutic importance." *Open Access Journal of Contraception* 6. (July 27, 2015): 105-115. doi: 10.2147/OAJC.S56400.

Wong, Chooi L, Cindy Farquahar, Helen Roberts, Michelle Proctor. "Oral contraceptive pill for primary dysmenorrhoea." Cochrane Database of Systematic Reviews 4, no. CD002120 (2009). https://doi.org/10.1002/14651858.CD002120.pub3.

EMERGENCY CONTRACEPTION (EC)

Bedsider. "Emergency contraception: the back-up plan." October 28, 2013. Video, 6:24. https://www.youtube.com/watch?v=Q2CEK2egMU0&t=9s&ab_channel=Bedsider.

Bedsider. "The Yuzpe method: Effective emergency contraception dating back to the '70s." Power to Decide. Last updated December 9, 2010. https://www.bedsider.org/features/88-the-yuzpe-method-effective-emergency-contraception-dating-back-to-the-70s.

Bosworth, MD, Michele C, Patti L. Olusola, MD, and Sarah B. Low, MD. "An Update on Emergency Contraception." *American Family Physician* 87, no. 7 (2014): 545-550.

Gemzell-Danielsson, Kristina. "Mechanism of action of emergency contraception." *Contraception* 82, no. 5 (2010): 404-409. https://doi.org/10.1016/j.contraception.2010.05.004.

Planned Parenthood Federation of America Inc. "Emergency Contraception." 2022. https://www.plannedparenthood.org/learn/morning-after-pill-emergency-contraception.

Power to Decide. "Bedsider." 2019. https://www.bedsider.org/birth-control/emergency_contraception.

Rosato, Elena, Manuela Farris, and Carlo Bastianelli. "Mechanism of Action of Ulipristal Acetate for Emergency Contraception: A Systematic Review." *Frontiers in Pharmacology* 6, no. 315 (2016). doi: 10.3389/fphar.2015.00315.

Vandergriendt, Carly, Laura Goldman, and Valinda Riggins Nwadike, MD, MPH. "How Often Can You Take Plan B and Other Emergency Contraceptive Pills?" Healthline. Last updated on July 28, 2020. https://www.healthline.com/health/healthy-sex/how-often-can-you-take-plan-b.

BARRIER METHODS

Bass Medical Group (blog). "Breast Pain: Why You May Need to Change Your Birth Control." 2022. https://www.bassmedicalgroup.com/blog-post/breast-pain-why-you-may-need-to-change-your-birth-control.

Centers for Disease Control and Prevention. "Condom Effectiveness: Female (Internal) Condom Use." U.S. Department of Health & Human Services. Last updated February 10, 2022. https://www.cdc.gov/condomeffectiveness/internal-condom-use.html.

CooperSurgical, Inc. "Milex Omniflex Style Diaphragm." 2022. https://www.coopersurgical.com/detail/milex-omniflex-style-diaphragm/.

Mayo Foundation for Medical Education and Research. "Cervical cap." 1998-2022. https://www.mayoclinic.org/tests-procedures/cervical-cap/about/pac-20393416.

Office on Women's Health in the Office of the Assistant Secretary for Health at the U.S. Department of Health and Human Services. "Sexually transmitted infections." June 11, 2019. https://www.womenshealth.gov/a-z-topics/sexually-transmitted-infections#:~:text=An%20STI%20is%20an%20infection,some%20STIs%20cannot%20be%20cured.

Planned Parenthood Federation of America Inc. "Cervical Cap." 2022. https://www.plannedparenthood.org/learn/birth-control/cervical-cap.

Power to Decide. "Bedsider." 2019. https://www.bedsider.org/birth-control.

THE PATCH AND THE RING

Galzote, Rosanna M, Sally Rafie, Rachel Teal, and Sheila K Mody. "Transdermal delivery of combined hormonal contraception: a review of the current literature." *International Journal of Women's Health* 9 (2017): 315-321. doi: 10.2147/IJWH.S102306.

Guida, Maurizio, Attilio Di Spiezio Sardo, Silvia Bramante, Stefania Sparice, Giuseppe Acunzo, Giovanni Antonio Tommaselli, Costantino Di Carlo, Massimiliano Pellicano, Elena Greco, Carmine Nappi. "Effects of two types of hormonal contraception—oral versus intravaginal—on the sexual life of women and their partners." *Human Reproduction* 20, no. 4 (2005): 1100-6. DOI: 10.1093/humrep/deh686.

Huang, Yongmei, Ruth B. Merkatz, Sharon L. Hillier, Kevin Roberts, Diana L. Blithe, Regine Sitruk-Ware, and Mitchell D. Creinin. "Effects of a One Year Reusable Contraceptive Vaginal Ring on Vaginal Microflora and the Risk of Vaginal Infection: An Open-Label Prospective Evaluation." *PLoS One* 10, no. 8 (2015): e0134460. doi: 10.1371/journal.pone.0134460.

pageninco. "My Birth Control Experience: NuvaRing vs. Pill | NuvaRing review, side effects and how to use." August 19, 2020. Video, 7:46. https://www.youtube.com/watch?v=N-HhMBxmze4k.

Planned Parenthood Federation of America Inc. "Birth Control Patch." 2022. https://www.plannedparenthood.org/learn/birth-control/birth-control-patch.

Power to Decide. "Bedsider: Birth control patch." 2019. https://www.bedsider.org/birth-control/the_patch.

Power to Decide. "Bedsider: Birth control ring." 2019. https://www.bedsider.org/birth-control/the_ring.

Roumen, Frans JME. "Review of the combined contraceptive vaginal ring, NuvaRing®." *Therapeutics and Clinical Risk Management* 4, no. 2 (2008): 441-451. doi: 10.2147/tcrm.s1964.

THE SHOT

Centers for Disease Control and Prevention. "Cancers Associated with HPV." Last updated December 13, 2021. https://www.cdc.gov/cancer/hpv/basic_info/cancers.htm#:~:text=Almost%20all%20cervical%20cancer%20is,cancer%20is%20caused%20by%20HPV.

Cimons, Marlene. "3-Month Contraceptive Shot Approved by FDA." *Los Angeles Times*, October 30, 1992. https://www.latimes.com/archives/la-xpm-1992-10-30-mn-984-story.html.

DeMaria, Andrea L, Beth Sundstrom, Stephanie Meier, Abigail Wiseley. "The myth of menstruation: how menstrual regulation and suppression impact contraceptive choice." *BMC Women's Health* 19, no. 1 (2019): 125. doi: 10.1186/s12905-019-0827-x.

Harel, Zeev, Christine Cole Johnson, Melanie A Gold, Barbara Cromer, Edward Peterson, Ronald Burkman, Margaret Stager, Robert Brown, Ann Bruner, Susan Coupey, Paige Hertweck, Henry Bone, Kevin Wolter, Anita Nelson, Sharon Marshall, Laura K Bachrach. "Recovery of bone mineral density in adolescents following the use of depot medroxyprogesterone acetate contraceptive injections." *Contraception* 81, no. 4 (2009): 281-91. DOI: 10.1016/j.contraception.2009.11.003.

Hubacher, David. "The Checkered History and Bright Future of Intrauterine Contraception in the United States." *Perspectives on Sexual and Reproductive Health* 34, no. 2 (2002): 98-103. DOI: https://doi.org/10.1363/3409802.

Kaiser Family Foundation. "DMPA Contraceptive Injection: Use and Coverage." Published January 29, 2020. https://www.kff.org/womens-health-policy/fact-sheet/dmpa-contraceptive-injection-use-and-coverage/.

Kaunitz, MD, Andrew. "Injectable Contraception." *The Global Library of Women's Medicines*, 2008. DOI 10.3843/GLOWM.10393.

Klitsch, M. "Injectable hormones and regulatory controversy: an end to the long-running story?" *Family Planning Perspec-*

tives 25, no. 1 (1993): 37-40. https://pubmed.ncbi.nlm.nih.gov/8432375/.

Lanza, Lee L, Lisa J McQuay, Kenneth J Rothman, Henry G Bone, Andrew M Kaunitz, Zeev Harel, Quazi Ataher, Douglas Ross, Philip L Arena, Kevin D Wolter. "Use of depot medroxyprogesterone acetate contraception and incidence of bone fracture." *Obstetrics and Gynecology* 121, no. 3 (2013): 593-600).

Leary, Warren E. "U.S. Approves Injectable Drug as Birth Control." *New York Times,* October 30, 1992. https://www.nytimes.com/1992/10/30/us/us-approves-injectable-drug-as-birth-control.html.

Lopez, Laureen M, Shanthi Ramesh, Mario Chen, Alison Edelman, Conrad Otterness, James Trussell, Frans M Helmerhorst. "Progestin-only contraceptives: effects on weight." Cochrane Database of Systematic Reviews 8, no. CD008815 (2016). doi: 10.1002/14651858.CD008815.pub4.

Mangan, Sharon A, Pamela G Larsen, Suzanne Hudson. "Overweight teens at increased risk for weight gain while using depot medroxyprogesterone acetate." *Journal of Pediatric and Adolescent Gynecology* 15, no. 2 (2002): 79-82. doi: 10.1016/s1083-3188(01)00147-4.

Meier, Christian, Yolanda B Brauchli, Susan S Jick, Marius E Kraenzlin, Christoph R Meier. "Use of depot medroxyprogesterone acetate and fracture risk." *Journal of Clinical Endocrinology and Metabolism* 95, no. 11 (2010): 4909-16. doi: 10.1210/jc.2010-0032.

Morse, MD, MPH, Jessica. "Depo SubQ: The do-it-yourself birth control shot." November 16, 2015. https://www.bedsider.org/features/789-depo-subq-the-do-it-yourself-birth-control-shot.

National Institute of Child Health and Human Development. "What are menstrual irregularities?" National Institute of Health. Last updated January 31, 2017. https://www.nichd.nih.gov/health/topics/menstruation/conditioninfo/irregularities.

NIH Osteoporosis and Related Bone Diseases - National Resource Center. "Bone Mass Measurement: What the Numbers Mean." October 2018. https://www.bones.nih.gov/health-info/bone/bone-health/bone-mass-measure.

NIH Osteoporosis and Related Bone Diseases - National Resource Center. "Pregnancy, Breastfeeding and Bone Health." December 2018. https://www.bones.nih.gov/health-info/bone/bone-health/pregnancy.

PBS. "A Timeline of Contraception." WGBH Educational Foundation: American Experience. 1996-2022. https://www.pbs.org/wgbh/americanexperience/features/pill-timeline/.

Power to Decide. "Bedsider: Birth control shot." 2019. https://www.bedsider.org/birth-control/the_shot.

Rademacher, Kate H, Jill Sergison, Laura Glich, Lauren Y Maldonado, Amelia Mackenzie, Geeta Nanda, Irina Yacobson. "Menstrual Bleeding Changes Are NORMAL: Proposed Counseling Tool to Address Common Reasons for Non-Use and

Discontinuation of Contraception." *Global Health: Science and Practice* 6, no. 3 (2018): 603-610. doi: 10.9745/GHSP-D-18-00093.

Renner, Regina Maria, Alison B Edelman, Andrew M Kaunitz. "Depot medroxyprogesterone acetate contraceptive injections and skeletal health." *Women's Health* 6, no. 3 (2010): 339-42. doi: 10.2217/whe.10.17.

Weisberg, Edith, and Ian S Fraser. "Contraception and endometriosis: challenges, efficacy, and therapeutic importance." *Open Access Journal of Contraception* 6 (2015): 105-115. doi: 10.2147/OAJC.S56400.

Westhoff, Carolyn. "Depot-medroxyprogesterone acetate injection (Depo-Provera): a highly effective contraceptive option with proven long-term safety." *Contraception* 68, no. 2 (2003): 75-87. doi: 10.1016/s0010-7824(03)00136-7.

World Health Organization. "Breast cancer and depot-medroxyprogesterone acetate: a multinational study. WHO Collaborative Study of Neoplasia and Steroid Contraceptives." *Lancet* 338, no. 8771 (1991): 833-8. https://pubmed.ncbi.nlm.nih.gov/1681212/.

THE IMPLANT

Abdel-Aleem, Hany. Catherine d'Arcangues, Kirsten M Vogelsong, Mary Lyn Gaffield, A Metin Gülmezoglu. "Treatment of vaginal bleeding irregularities induced by progestin only contraceptives." Cochrane Database of Systematic Reviews no. 10 (2013): CD003449. doi: 10.1002/14651858.CD003449.pub5.

Centers for Disease Control. "Contraception." January 13, 2022. https://www.cdc.gov/reproductivehealth/contraception/index.htm.

Kaiser Family Foundation. "Contraceptive Implants." Published on October 1, 2019. https://www.kff.org/womens-health-policy/fact-sheet/contraceptive-implants/.

Mansour, Diana, Tjeerd Korver, Maya Marintcheva-Petrova, Ian S Fraser. "The effects of Implanon on menstrual bleeding patterns." The European Journal of Reproductive Health Care 13, no. 1 (2008): 13-28. DOI: 10.1080/13625180801959931.

Organon. "What is NEXPLANON?" Accessed on February 20, 2022. https://www.nexplanon.com/what-is-nexplanon/.

HORMONAL IUDS

Bayer. "Frequently asked questions about Mirena." Last modified January 4, 2022. https://www.mirena-us.com/about-mirena/faqs.

Bayer HealthCare Pharmaceuticals. "Mirena®." Updated July 2008. https://www.accessdata.fda.gov/drugsatfda_docs/label/2008/021225s019lbl.pdf.

Beaton, Caroline. "Why Does America Have Fewer Types of IUDs Than Other Countries?" *The Atlantic,* April 18, 2017. https://www.theatlantic.com/health/archive/2017/04/why-america-has-fewer-iuds-than-other-countries/523077/.

Burnette, Brandon R. "Comstock Act of 1873 (1873)." *The First Amendment Encyclopedia*, Middle Tennessee State University. 2009. https://www.mtsu.edu/first-amendment/article/1038/comstock-act-of-1873.

Hubacher, David. "The Checkered History and Bright Future of Intrauterine Contraception in the United States." *Perspectives on Sexual and Reproductive Health* 34, no. 2 (2002): 98-103. DOI: https://doi.org/10.1363/3409802.

Kailasam, Chandra, and David Cahill. "Review of the safety, efficacy and patient acceptability of the levonorgestrel-releasing intrauterine system." Dovepress Patient Preference and Adherence no. 2 (2008): 293-302. doi: 10.2147/ppa.s3464.

Lanzola, Emily L and Kari Ketvertis. "Intrauterine Device." Treasure Island: StatPearls [Internet], 2021. https://www.ncbi.nlm.nih.gov/books/NBK557403/.

Margulies, MD, Lazar. "History of Intrauterine Devices." *Bulletin of the New York Academy of Medicine* 51, no. 5 (1975): 662-667. https://www.ncbi.nlm.nih.gov/pmc/articles/PMC1749527/pdf/bullnyacadmed00161-0098.pdf.

Medicines 360. "Medicines360, Afaxys Partner to Expand Public Health Access to LILETTA® (levonorgestrel-releasing intrauterine system) 52mg." September 6, 2018. https://www.medicines360.org/2018/09/06/medicines360-afaxys-partner-to-expand-public-health-access-to-liletta-levonorgestrel-releasing-intrauterine-system-52-mg/.

Nahum, Gerard G, Andrew M Kaunitz, Kimberly Rosen, Thomas Schmelter, Richard Lynen. "Ovarian cysts: presence and persistence with use of a 13.5mg levonorgestrel-releasing intrauterine system." *Contraception* 91, no. 5 (2015): 412-7. doi: 10.1016/j.contraception.2015.01.021.Epub.

Office on Women's Health in the Office of the Assistant Secretary for Health at the U.S. Department of Health and Human Services. "Birth control methods." Last updated February 14, 2019. https://www.womenshealth.gov/a-z-topics/birth-control-methods.

PBS. "Birth Control Before the Pill." WGBH Educational Foundation: American Experience. 1996-2022. https://www.pbs.org/wgbh/americanexperience/features/pill-birth-control-pill/.

Population Council, Inc. "Our History." 2022. https://www.popcouncil.org/about/timeline.

Power to Decide. "Bedsider." 2019. https://www.bedsider.org/methods/iud.

Reproductive Health Access Project (blog). "A History: the IUD." January 17, 2013. https://www.reproductiveaccess.org/2013/01/a-history-the-iud/.

Ross, Elisa K and Medhi Kebria. "Incidental ovarian cysts: When to reassure, when to reassess, when to refer." *Cleveland Clinic Journal of Medicine* 80, no. 8 (2013): 503-14. doi: 10.3949/ccjm.80a.12155.

Scully, Simone and Valinda Riggins Nwadike, MD, MPH. "Everything You Need to Know About IUD Insertion." Healthline. Published on April 28, 2021. https://www.healthline.com/health/birth-control/iud-insertion.

Sonfield, Adam. "Popularity Disparity: Attitudes About the IUD in Europe and the United States." *Guttmacher Policy Review* 10, no. 4 (2007). https://www.guttmacher.org/gpr/2007/11/popularity-disparity-attitudes-about-iud-europe-and-united-states.

University Health Services: Tang Center. "Levonorgestrel IUDs: Mirena, Kyleena and Skyla." University of California, Berkeley. June 27, 2019. http://uhs.berkeley.edu/sites/default/files/iud_hormonal.pdf.

Weisburg, Edith and Ian S. Fraser. "Contraception and endometriosis: challenges, efficacy, and therapeutic importance." *Open Access Journal of Contraception* 6. (July 27, 2015): 105-115. doi: 10.2147/OAJC.S56400.

THE COPPER IUD

Centers for Disease Control. "Contraception." January 13, 2022. https://www.cdc.gov/reproductivehealth/contraception/index.htm.

CooperSurgical, Inc. "Meet the Paragard IUD." Paragard® intrauterine copper contraceptive. October 2021. https://www.paragard.com.

Kaiser Family Foundation. "Contraceptive Implants." Published on October 1, 2019. https://www.kff.org/womens-health-policy/fact-sheet/contraceptive-implants/.

Kaneshiro, Bliss, and Tod Aeby. "Long-term safety, efficacy, and patient acceptability of the intrauterine Copper T-380A contraceptive device." *International Journal of Women's Health* no. 2 (2010): 211-220. doi: 10.2147/ijwh.s6914.

Luchowski, Alicia T, Britta L Anderson, Michael L Power, Greta B Raglan, Eve Espey, Jay Schulkin. "Obstetrician-gynecologists and contraception: long-acting reversible contraception practices and education." *Contraception* 89, no. 6 (2014): 578-83. doi: 10.1016/j.contraception.2014.02.004.Epub.

Margulies, MD, Lazar. "History of Intrauterine Devices." *Bulletin of the New York Academy of Medicine* 51, no. 5 (1975): 662-667. https://www.ncbi.nlm.nih.gov/pmc/articles/PMC1749527/pdf/bullnyacadmed00161-0098.pdf.

Office on Women's Health in the Office of the Assistant Secretary for Health at the U.S. Department of Health and Human Services. "Birth control methods." Last updated February 14, 2019. https://www.womenshealth.gov/a-z-topics/birth-control-methods.

Population Council, Inc. "Our History." 2022. https://www.popcouncil.org/about/timeline.

Power to Decide. "Bedsider." 2019. https://www.bedsider.org/birth-control/emergency_contraception.

Ray, DNP, Laurie and Kate Wahl. "IUD myths and misconceptions." Clue by Biowink GmbH. 2022. https://helloclue.com/articles/sex/iuds-myths-misconceptions-insertion-pain-infection.

The American College of Obstetricians and Gynecologists Committee on Gynecologic Practice. "Increasing Access to Contraceptive Implants and Intrauterine Devices to Reduce Unintended Pregnancy." Committee Opinion, no. 642 (Oct 2015). https://www.acog.org/clinical/clinical-guidance/committee-opinion/articles/2015/10/increasing-access-to-contraceptive-implants-and-intrauterine-devices-to-reduce-unintended-pregnancy.

Tight, Claire. "IUD Expulsion: Is it as scary as it sounds?" Bedsider. Published January 26, 2015. https://www.bedsider.org/features/643-iud-expulsion-is-it-as-scary-as-it-sounds.

STERILIZATION

Amory, John K. "Development of Novel Male Contraceptives." Clinical Translational Science 13, no. 2 (2020): 228-237. doi: 10.1111/cts.12708.

Anawalt, Bradley D., Mara Y. Roth, Jonas Ceponis, Vijaya Surampadi, John K. Amory, Ronald S. Swerdloff, Peter Y. Liu, Clint Dart, William J. Bremner, Régine Sitruk-Ware, Narender Kumar, Diana Blithe, Stephanie T. Page, Christina Wang. "Combined Nestorone–testosterone gel suppresses serum gonadotropins to concentrations associated with effective hormonal contraception in men." *Andrology* 7, no. 6 (2019): 878-887. https://doi.org/10.1111/andr.12603.

Attardi, Barbara J, Brett T Marck, Alvin M Matsumoto, Sailaja Koduri, Sheri A Hild. "Long-term effects of dimethandrolone 17β-undecanoate and 11β-methyl-19-nortestosterone 17β-dodecylcarbonate on body composition, bone mineral density, serum gonadotropins, and androgenic/anabolic activity in castrated male rats." *Journal of Andrology* 32, no. 2 (2011): 183-92. doi: 10.2164/jandrol.110.010371.

Bayer. "Essure: permanent birth control." Essure. Last updated January 13, 2020. https://www.essure.com/.

Chappell, Bill. "California's Prison Sterilizations Reportedly Echo Eugenics Era." *NPR: The Two-Way*, July 9, 2013. https://www.npr.org/sections/thetwo-way/2013/07/09/200444613/californias-prison-sterilizations-reportedly-echoes-eugenics-era.

Cohen, Adam. *Imbeciles: The Supreme Court, American Eugenics, and the Sterilization of Carrie Buck.* New York: Penguin Books, 2017.

Curtis, Kathryn M, Anshu P Mohllajee, Herbert B Peterson. "Regret following female sterilization at a young age: a systematic review." *Contraception* 73, no. 2 (2005): 205-10. DOI: 10.1016/j.contraception.2005.08.006.

Eberhardt, Judith, Anna van Welsch, Neil Meikle. "Attitudes toward the male contraceptive pill in men and women in casual and stable sexual relationships." *Journal of Family Plan-*

ning and Reproductive Health Care 35, no. 5 (2009) 161-5. doi: 10.1783/147118909788707986.

Friedman, M, L Nickels, D Sokal, A Hamlin, G King, D Levine, H Vahdat, K Shane. "Interest Among U.S. Men for New Male Contraceptive Options: Consumer Research Study." Male Contraceptive Initiative. February 2019. https://www.male-contraceptive.org/uploads/1/3/1/9/131958006/mci_consumerresearchstudy.pdf.

Grady, WR, K Tanfer, JO Billy, J Lincoln-Hanson. "Men's perceptions of their roles and responsibilities regarding sex, contraception and childrearing." *Family Planning Perspectives* 28, no. 5 (1996): 221-6. https://pubmed.ncbi.nlm.nih.gov/8886765/.

Heinemann, Klaas, Farid Saad, Martin Wiesemes, Steven White, Lothar Heinemann. "Attitudes toward male fertility control: results of a multinational survey on four continents." *Human Reproduction* 20, no. 2 (2005): 549-556. https://academic.oup.com/humrep/article/20/2/549/603220.

Herrel, Lindsey A, Michael Goodman, Marc Goldstein, Wayland Hsiao. "Outcomes of Microsurgical Vasovasostomy for Vasectomy Reversal: A Meta-analysis and Systematic Review." *Infertility* 85, no. 4 (2015): 819-825. https://doi.org/10.1016/j.urology.2014.12.023.

Kim, SH, CJ Shin, JG Kim, SY Moon, JY Lee, YS Chang. "Microsurgical reversal of tubal sterilization: a report on 1,118 cases." *Fertility and Sterility* 68, no. 5 (1997): 865-70. https://pubmed.ncbi.nlm.nih.gov/9389817/.

Lalonde, Dianne. "Sexist barriers block women's choice to be sterilized." *The Conversation,* August 14, 2018. https://the-conversation.com/sexist-barriers-block-womens-choice-to-be-sterilized-99754.

Meriggiola, MC and WJ Bremner. "Progestin-androgen combination regimens for male contraception." *Journal of Andrology* 18, no. 3 (1997): 240-4. https://pubmed.ncbi.nlm.nih.gov/9203050/.

McEvoy, Jemima. "Pelosi Calls For Investigation Into Claims Of Mass Hysterectomies, Poor Covid-19 Care At ICE Detention Center." *Forbes,* September 15, 2020. https://www.forbes.com/sites/jemimamcevoy/2020/09/15/pelosi-calls-for-investigation-into-claims-of-mass-hysterectomies-poor-covid-19-care-at-ice-detention-center/?sh=77c5d0ff5f7c.

Parsemus Foundation. "Male Contraception Attitudes: Summary of Surveys and Research." March 2016. https://www.parsemus.org/wp-content/uploads/2016/03/Male-Contraception-Attitudes-Surveys-and-Research-7-8-16.pdf.

Power to Decide. "Bedsider." 2019. https://www.bedsider.org/birth-control/sterilization.

Reilly, Philip. "Eugenics and Involuntary Sterilization: 1907–2015." *Annual Review of Genomics and Human Genetics* 16 (2015): 351-68. https://pubmed.ncbi.nlm.nih.gov/26322647/.

Sofair, AN and LC Kaldjian. "Eugenic sterilization and a qualified Nazi analogy: the United States and Germany, 1930-1945."

Annals of Internal Medicine 132, no. 4: 312-9. https://pubmed.
ncbi.nlm.nih.gov/10681287/.

The American College of Obstetricians and Gynecologists.
"Sterilization by Laparoscopy." August 2019. https://www.
acog.org/womens-health/faqs/sterilization-by-laparoscopy.

The American College of Obstetricians and Gynecologists.
"Sterilization for Women and Men." Published March 2019.
https://www.acog.org/womens-health/faqs/steriliza-
tion-for-women-and-men.

Thirumalai, Arthi, Jonas Ceponis, John K Amory, Ronald Swerdloff, Vijaya Surampudi, Peter Y Liu, William J Bremner, Eric
Harvey, Diana L Blithe, Min S Lee, Laura Hull, Christina
Wang, Stephanie T Page. "Effects of 28 Days of Oral Dimethandrolone Undecanoate in Healthy Men: A Prototype Male
Pill." *Journal of Clinical Endocrinology and Metabolism* 104, no.
2 (2019): 423-432. doi: 10.1210/jc.2018-01452.

Turner, Leo, Ann J Conway, Mark Jimenez, Peter Y Liu, Elise
Forbes, Robert I McLachlan, David J Handelsman. "Contraceptive efficacy of a depot progestin and androgen combination in men." *Journal of Clinical Endocrinology and Metabolism*
88, no. 10 (2003): 4659-67. doi: 10.1210/jc.2003-030107.

van Seeters, Jacoba AH, Su Jen Chua, Bên WJ Mol, Carolien
AM Koks. "Tubal anastomosis after previous sterilization:
a systematic review." *Human Reproduction Update* 23, no. 3
(2017): 358-370. doi: 10.1093/humupd/dmx003.

von Eckardstein, Sigrid, Gabriela Noe, Vivian Brache, Eberhard Nieschlag, Horacio Croxatto, Francisco Alvarez, Alfred Moo-Young, Irving Sivin, Narender Kumar, Margaret Small, Kalyan Sundaram, International Committee for Contraception Research, The Population Council. "A clinical trial of 7 alpha-methyl-19-nortestosterone implants for possible use as a long-acting contraceptive for men." *Journal of Clinical Endocrinology and Metabolism* 88, no. 11 (2003): 5232-9. doi: 10.1210/jc.2002-022043.

Waller, Donald, David Block, Elaine Lissner, Christopher Premanandan, Gary Gamerman. "Reversibility of Vasalgel™ male contraceptive in a rabbit model." *Basic and Clinical Andrology* 27 (2017): 8. doi: 10.1186/s12610-017-0051-1.

Wardell, D. "Margaret Sanger: birth control's successful revolutionary." *American Journal of Public Health* 70, no. 7 (1980): 736-742. doi: 10.2105/ajph.70.7.736.

Weissman, Alanna "How Doctors Fail Women Who Don't Want Children." *New York Times,* November 11, 2017. https://www.nytimes.com/2017/11/30/sunday-review/women-sterilization-children-doctors.html.

World Health Organization Task Force on Methods for the Regulation of Male Fertility. "Contraceptive efficacy of testosterone-induced azoospermia and oligozoospermia in normal men." *Fertility and Sterility* 65, no. 4 (1996): 821-9. https://pubmed.ncbi.nlm.nih.gov/8654646/.

World Health Organization Task Force on Methods for the Regulation of Male Fertility. "Contraceptive efficacy of testosterone-induced azoospermia in normal men." *The Lancet* 336, no. 8721 (1990): 955-959. https://doi.org/10.1016/0140-6736(90)92416-F.

ZOOM OUT

Ahmed, Zara. "The Unprecedented Expansion of the Global Gag Rule: Trampling Rights, Health and Free Speech." *Guttmacher Policy Review* 23 (2020). https://www.guttmacher.org/gpr/2020/04/unprecedented-expansion-global-gag-rule-trampling-rights-health-and-free-speech.

Bedsider. "SILCS: It's not your mama's diaphragm (not her spermicide, either)." Power to Decide. Last updated July 20, 2015. https://www.bedsider.org/features/159-silcs-it-s-not-your-mama-s-diaphragm-not-her-spermicide-either.

Cunningham, Paige Winfield. "ACA's confusing birth control rules." *Politico,* July 23, 2013. https://www.politico.com/story/2013/07/aca-birth-control-rule-creates-confusion-094573.

Demissie, PhD, Zewditu, Nancy D Bremner, PhD, Tim McManus, MS, Shari L. Shanklin, MPH, Joseph Hawkins, MA, Laura Kann, PhD. *School Health Profiles 2014: Characteristics of Health Programs Among Secondary Schools.* Center for Disease Control and Prevention. 2015. https://www.cdc.gov/healthyyouth/data/profiles/pdf/2014/2014_profiles_report.pdf.

Foster, Diana Greene, Denis Hulett, Mary Bradsberry, Philip Darney, Michael Policar. "Number of oral contraceptive pill packages dispensed and subsequent unintended pregnancies." *Obstetrics and Gynecology* 117, no. 3 (2011): 566-72. doi: 10.1097/AOG.0b013e3182056309.

Frederiksen, Brittni, Usha Ranji, Alina Salganicoff, Michelle Long. "Women's Sexual and Reproductive Health Services: Key Findings from the 2020 KFF Women's Health Survey." April 21, 2021. https://www.kff.org/womens-health-policy/issue-brief/womens-sexual-and-reproductive-health-services-key-findings-from-the-2020-kff-womens-health-survey/.

Frost, Jennifer J, Jennifer Mueller, and Zoe H. Pleasure. "Trends and Differentials in Receipt of Sexual and Reproductive Health Services in the United States: Services Received and Sources of Care, 2006–2019." Guttmacher Institute. DOI: https://doi.org/10.1363/2021.33017.

Ginsburg, Ruther Bader. "THE SUPREME COURT; Excerpts from Senate Hearing on the Ginsburg Nomination." *The New York Times,* July 22, 1993. https://www.nytimes.com/1993/07/22/us/the-supreme-court-excerpts-from-senate-hearing-on-the-ginsburg-nomination.html.

Grady, William R, John OG Billy, Daniel H Klepinger. "Contraceptive Method Switching in the United States." *Perspectives on Sexual and Reproductive Health* 34, no. 3. (2002): 135-145. DOI: https://doi.org/10.1363/3413502.

Guttmacher Institute: State Laws and Policies. "Insurance Coverage of Contraceptives." Last updated January 1, 2022. https://www.guttmacher.org/state-policy/explore/insurance-coverage-contraceptives.

Guttmacher Institute: State Laws and Policies. "Sex and HIV Education." Last updated January 1, 2022. https://www.guttmacher.org/state-policy/explore/sex-and-hiv-education.

Guttmacher Institute. "The Federal Contraceptive Coverage Guarantee: An Effective Policy That Should Be Strengthened and Expanded." June 2021. https://www.guttmacher.org/fact-sheet/contraceptive-coverage-guarantee.

Lindberg, PhD, Laura Duberstein, Isaac Maddow-Zimet, Heather Boonstra, MA. "Changes in Adolescents' Receipt of Sex Education, 2006–2013." *Journal of Adolescent Health* 58, no. 6 (2016): 621-627. https://doi.org/10.1016/j.jadohealth.2016.02.004.

Millhiser, Ian. "The Supreme Court just gave Republicans a powerful new weapon against Obamacare." *Vox,* July 8, 2020. https://www.vox.com/2020/7/8/21317323/supreme-court-obamacare-little-sisters-clarence-thomas-pennsylvania-birth-control.

National Institutes of Health: National Institute of Allergy and Infectious Diseases. "Vaginal ring for HIV prevention receives positive opinion from European regulator." News Releases. July 24, 2020. https://www.nih.gov/news-events/news-releases/vaginal-ring-hiv-prevention-receives-positive-opinion-european-regulator.

Secura, PhD, MPH, Gina, Jenifer E. Allsworth, PhD, Tessa Madden, MD, MPH, Jennifer L. Mullersman, BSN, and Jeffrey F. Peipert, MD, PhD. "The Contraceptive CHOICE Project: Reducing Barriers to Long-Acting Reversible Contraception." *American Journal of Obstetrics and Gynecology* 203, no. 2 (2010). doi: 10.1016/j.ajog.2010.04.017.

SIECUS: National Guidelines Task Force. *Guidelines for Comprehensive Sexuality Education: Kindergarten-12th Grade, 3rd ed.* Meadville: Fulton Press, 2004.

Sonfield, Adam. "A Fragmented System: Ensuring Comprehensive Contraceptive Coverage in All U.S. Health Insurance Plans." *Guttmacher Policy Review* 24 (February 2021). https://www.guttmacher.org/gpr/2021/02/fragmented-system-ensuring-comprehensive-contraceptive-coverage-all-us-health-insurance.

Sonfield, Adam. "'Refusal of Care' Rule Provides Potent New Tools to Deny Health Care and Discriminate Against Patients." Guttmacher Institute: Policy Analysis. May 3, 2019. https://www.guttmacher.org/article/2019/05/refusal-care-rule-provides-potent-new-tools-deny-health-care-and-discriminate.

Sonfield, Adam. "Uninsured Rate for People of Reproductive Age Ticked Up Between 2016 and 2019." Guttmacher Institute: Policy Analysis. April 1, 2021. https://www.guttmacher.org/article/2021/04/uninsured-rate-people-reproductive-age-ticked-between-2016-and-2019.

Zolna, Mia, Sean Finn, Jennifer Frost. "Memorandum: Estimating the impact of changes in the Title X network on patient capacity." Guttmacher Institute. Last updated February 26, 2020. https://www.guttmacher.org/sites/default/files/article_files/estimating_the_impact_of_changes_in_the_title_x_network_on_patient_capacity_2.pdf.

ZOOM IN

Harper, Cynthia C, Corinne H Rocca, Kirsten M Thompson, Johanna Morfesis, Suzan Goodman, Philip D Darney, Carolyn L Westhoff, J Joseph Speidel. "Reductions in pregnancy rates in the USA with long-acting reversible contraception: a cluster randomised trial." *The Lancet* 386, no. 9993(2015): 562-8. doi: 10.1016/S0140- 6736(14)62460-0.

Lee, Jessica K, Sara M Parisi, Aletha Y Akers, Sonya Borrero, Eleanor Bimla Schwarz. "The impact of contraceptive counseling in primary care on contraceptive use." *Journal of General Internal Medicine* 26, no. 7 (2011): 731-6. doi: http://dx.doi.org/10.1007/s11606-011-1647-3.

Planned Parenthood Federation of America Inc. "Tips for Talking." 2022. https://www.plannedparenthood.org/learn/parents/tips-talking.

Planned Parenthood Federation of America, Inc. and New York University's Center for Latino Adolescent and Family Health. "Parents and Teens Talk about Sexuality: A National Survey." 2014. https://www.plannedparenthood.org/uploads/filer_public/ac/50/ac50c2f7-cbc9-46b7-8531-ad3e92712016/nationalpoll_09-14_v2_1.pdf.

Schwarz, Eleanor Bimla, Sara M Parisi, Sanithia L Williams, Grant J Shevchik, Rachel Hess. "Promoting safe prescribing in primary care with a contraceptive vital sign: a cluster-randomized controlled trial." *Annals of Family Medicine* 10, no. 6 (2012): 516-22. doi: 10.1370/afm.1404.

Women's Preventive Services Initiative—Multidisciplinary Steering Committee. *Recommendations for Preventive Services for Women: Final Report to the U.S. Department of Health and Human Services, Health Resources &Services Administration.* Washington, DC: American College of Obstetricians and Gynecologists, 2017. https://www.womenspreventivehealth.org/wp-content/uploads/WPSI_2016FullReport.pdf.